D1435705

OFFICIALLY DISCARDED BY
UNIVERSITY OF PITTSBURGH LIBRARY

CUBA and the USA:

A New World Order?

Notice in Florida to birds flying south.

You are advised to avoid Cuba,
the island 90 miles from here,
the former pearl of the Antilles.
It will appear beautiful and welcome as a landfall,
but you are advised to overfly it to Jamaica;
In order to avoid its very detrimental
communistic atmospheres and
non-exclusive feeding and resting grounds
where you may find yourself
in the company of
Cuban birds
of most dubious persuasions.

Bob Randolph

CUBA

and the USA:

A New World Order?

Harry R. Targ

International Publishers　　　*New York*

Cover photos:

**Havana, 1990 and a scene from
a day care center, Havana**

© 1992 International Publishers Co., New York
1st printing, 1992
Manufactured in the United States of America

Library of Congress Cataloging-in-Publication Data

Targ, Harry R.
    Cuba and the USA : a new world order? / Harry R. Targ.
        p.   cm.
    Includes bibliographical references and index.
    ISBN 0-7178-0700-2 : $5.50
    1. United States--Foreign relations--Cuba. 2. Cuba--Foreign
relations--United States. 3. Cuba--History--Revolution, 1959-
-Influence. 4. Cuba--Politics and government--1959-   I. Title.
E183.8.C9T37   1992
327.7307291--dc20   92-5771
                                                            CIP

CONTENTS

Bob Randolph is author of *Cuba Poems, June 1991,* and *I Am Writing
of Hand Grenades, Butterflies and Kisses* (Berkeley, 1991).

v

Yo estoy acostumbrada.

We are small and proud
but the giant exhausts us
by lying on our shoulders,
pressing so we hardly breathe
gripping our throats
while we were singing;
turning off the lights while we dance
shouting in a foreign tongue
while we are quietly in each other's arms—
Accusing us on the telephone at 3 AM
of disturbing the peace.

Yo estoy acostumbrada ahora,
pero yo no estaba acostumbrada antes.

You colossus,
you steal our spare parts from our trade,
steal our needs,
our pencils, our postcards,
our human values
with deadly threats,
with violent movies
and perfume ads for our young,
scoffing at our good will,
digging up our roads,
our lives
to waste ourselves defending our lovely island
against you.
What have we done to you except be resentful
of your seizure of us when
we had the Spaniards on their knees?
and you blew up your battleship
in our harbor to move inside our world,
then with Machado and Batista

you tore our hopes out by the roots
and finally—
made us fight to be ourselves—
and now?
Again you menace us
with your cosmic weapons to make us
live in terror of your American fears,
your terrors—out of control.

Yes, yo estoy acostumbrada.
 Yo tengo que decir a Uds.,

estoy acostumbrada a Uds.

Bob Randolph

Young agricultural workers in Cuba

ACKNOWLEDGEMENTS

I wish to express appreciation to a number of persons who have made it possible for me to visit and study the Cuban Revolution. Professor Cliff DuRand of Morgan State University and Professor Robert Stone of Long Island University have assumed the major burdens of organizing each year's conference for the Radical Philosophy Association. Their efforts have been extraordinary and reflect their deep commitment to the Cuban people, to engaged scholarship, and international understanding.

Our Cuban hosts have been warm and generous in their efforts to improve our understanding of the Cuban revolution and to provide us with the freedom to explore its strengths and weaknesses. Dean Antonio Toledo believes in the value that dialogue and debate between scholars can have in reducing hostilities and improving the human condition. Professor Thalia Fung has a burning commitment to the humanist values of the Cuban revolution and the role that philosophy can play in furthering the achievement of those values.

Several translators, teachers at the foreign language institute, provided us with valuable insights into the revolution through their giving of time to answer endless questions: Raul Rodriguez, Eduardo Lorenzo, Reynaldo Verrier, and Carlos Gonzalez Chavez.

Many persons spent hours telling us about the Cuba they know and love, and instilled that love in their listeners: Karen Wald, Marc Frank, Carlos Tablada, Juan Antonio Blanco, and Fernando Garcia.

Lastly, the Cuban people who struggle to keep their revolution alive in the face of enormous odds serve as a particular inspiration at a time when progressive forces around the world have suffered great losses. They inspire progressives to work all the harder to overcome the economic embargo and military aggression from our country against their island nation.

Finally, as always, I am personally indebted to Dena Targ, Rebecca Targ, Genevieve Targ, Marlene Targ Brill, and, in memory, to Irving Targ.

Harry R. Targ

Chapter 1

Cuba as Reality and Metaphor

The Cuban Revolution as Reality:

An Introduction

Cuban history is replete with revolutionary ferment as land-owners, slaves, workers, peasants, students—nationalists all—sought to establish the freedom and self-determination that comported with the historical circumstances they experienced. The most dramatic revolution, of course, was the one sparked by a small band of guerrilla fighters in the 1950s led by Fidel Castro, ousting U.S.-sponsored dictator, Fulgencio Batista from power. Then over the next thirty years, Cuban society was transformed into a socialist state infused with values of equality and popular power.

Before 1959, Cuba, while relatively developed by Latin American standards, was a country of enormous differences in wealth and power. Small numbers of Cuban landowners, business persons, and government officials lived well, while the vast majority of the Cuban people, particularly those living outside Havana, lived in poverty. The country's economy was dominated by United States investors and gangsters. Havana, with about ten per cent of the Cuban population, was one of the grand sin capitals of the world, dominated by gambling and prostitution and designed to service the needs of North American tourists. Hence, Cubans saw around them islands of sumptuous glitter in a sea of squalor.

1

How the Cuba of the 1950s came to be like this requires an examination of Cuba's experience of Spanish conquest and colonialism and United States neo-colonial control of the island's economy, an economy structured around the production and export of sugar, beginning in the sixteenth century, and tourism flowering after World War II. The Cuban story in brief is one of domination, subordination, and the struggle for national self-determination. These contending forces link early slave revolts to landowner rebellions against Spanish dominance of the economy, to Cuba's continuing struggle to maintain its increasingly threatened independence in the 1990s.

After Batista was defeated, the new Cuban regime began the process of rectifying the inequities in Cuban life. The Agrarian Reform law of May 1959, followed by a succession of refinements over the years, sought to guarantee every Cuban access to land and to limit the amount of land any individual, Cuban or foreign, could own. The Cubans launched a literacy campaign to teach everyone to read and write. They initiated health care programs that would eventually be world renowned. They also initiated what have become never-ending debates about how the economic life of the country should be organized, particularly the extent to which moral or material incentives should govern the behavior of Cuban workers.

Internationally, Cuba began to play a role well in excess of its power capabilities and geographic position for reasons of principle and pragmatism. As to principle, Cubans saw themselves in solidarity with all other Third World peoples who had experienced colonialism and neo-colonialism. And since their revolution was born in guerrilla struggle, the Cubans were willing to offer their modest support to other peoples engaged in struggles for liberation. The solidarity was particularly strong with Cuba's Latin American brothers and sisters and with Africans. In both cases, there was a cultural as well as ideological affinity.

While the Cubans did selectively support revolutionary groups in the Third World, they also began to provide non-military assistance to new governments. As the Cubans trained their own doctors and developed a sophisticated medical system, they increasingly sent health care workers to Africa, Latin America, and the Caribbean to train others. Cubans with other skills, too, were sent to various countries to help in the process of economic development.

The spirit of international solidarity between Cubans and other peoples has been strong. It has been reinforced over the years since 1959 by practical considerations as well. The path of national autonomy and socialist development incurred the wrath of the United States, and Cuban foreign policy was increasingly premised upon the assumption that international solidarity would lead to a bloc of nations that would act together to limit the hegemonic designs of the USA. Along with military and non-military support for allies, Cuba, by the 1970s, became active in the non-aligned movement, an effort by Third World countries to coordinate their political and economic activities to create more leverage against the powerful and rich nations. The non-aligned movement assumed that the most fundamental dimension of conflict in the international system was not that between East and West (the Soviet Union and the United States) but rather between North and South (the rich countries of the North against the poor countries of the South).

As has been hinted at, perhaps the most fundamental reality of the Cuban revolution has been the sustained hostility of the United States. The Eisenhower Administration was suspicious of the tiny band of guerrillas organizing in the Sierra Maestra mountains and after that movement seized power, the United States government moved quickly to challenge Cuba's radical reformism. The Cubans responded in kind and consequently the period from 1959 to 1961 was one of escalating tensions and hostilities characterized by the U.S. installation of an economic blockade and the failed effort to invade and overthrow the Cuban revolution at the Bay of Pigs. The Cubans, for their part, pushed ahead to create a socialist economy and as access to their traditional economic partners was closed they established close ties with the Soviet Union. Thus a revolution that was the latest phase of a 400-year drive to national self-determination became enveloped in the Cold War. The real issue between the United States and Cuba was who would control Cuba's economic and political life, the Colossus of the North or the tiny island nation itself.

The Cuban Revolution as Metaphor

The Cuban revolution has generated changes for the Cuban people, led to a policy of international activism not seen before 1959, and involved its people, by virtue of U.S. hostility, to a thirty-year confrontation with the United States. Scholars and political actors can argue about the virtues or failures of the Cuban revolution but neither can deny the impacts that it has had on peoples in Cuba, the Third World, and the United States.

The Cuban revolution has meaning at another level of human experience. It is as a metaphor or symbolic representation of the possibilities of human potential that the revolution has affected peoples all over the world.

First, for many of the generation of U.S. citizens coming of age in the late 1950s and 1960s, the successful guerrilla war led by a band of scruffy doctors, lawyers, students, peasants, and workers inspired movements seeking to transform U.S. society itself. The Cuban revolution represented to young Americans the possibility of the young, the weak, the disenfranchised, the disadvantaged seizing history and reworking society in the direction of equality and human liberation. The images of Fidel Castro, Che Guevara, and Camilo Cienfuegos were juxtaposed in the minds of many young Americans with the images of Dwight Eisenhower, John Foster Dulles, Allen Dulles, Joseph McCarthy and others who were instrumental in the socio-economic system of the 1950s, a decade of repression and reaction.

Perhaps the mythology (and reality) of Che Guevara most inspired the generation of the 1960s in the industrial capitalist world. Che was a man who gave up his privileges as a middle class Argentinean and trained doctor to fight for the poor and oppressed. After the Cuban revolutionaries seized state power and the revolution began to be institutionalized, Che moved on to Africa and finally Bolivia to fight the good fight for revolutionary change. While he was ultimately killed by the Bolivian military aided by U.S. advisers, his persona represented the alternative to possessive individualism, consumerism, and Social Darwinism reflected in the institutions, policies, economic processes, and culture in the bourgeois world.

The power of Che was not derived only from his guerrilla heroics. In the 1960s he posited the possibility of creating the

"New Man" (of course he should have spoken about "the new human being" but even this towering figure of the revolution had not transcended the sexism of his time and place). This new person, ultimately a product of a new kind of society, would have a consciousness that was social; that saw the needs of the community as the most important in one's life. The new society was not one in which each competed and struggled against all but rather one in which the welfare of each person depended upon the welfare of all.

The concrete manifestation of Che's philosophy in Cuba was the great debate in the 1960s (it never really ended) between moral and material incentives. Capitalist production relations are based upon the premise that people work because they will gain materially from the activity; that is, they will earn a wage. In wealthier societies, workers are offered not merely self-sustenance for their labor but the faint possibility of real wealth. Modern capitalist societies are driven by "Fordism;" mass production and mass consumption, satisfying wants generated by the manipulation of people's consciousness.

For "the New Man," productive activity occurs for the purpose of achieving an improved quality of life for the population at large. Workers are motivated by the desire to achieve the goals of the revolution: improve education, health care, housing, increase the availability of food etc. Each person works for the good of the whole, not for the satisfaction of artificially created needs for each individual worker. Ultimately, the new society must break the link between jobs and income. Workers work for the revolution; i.e., for the public good.

The policy implications of adopting moral or material incentives would be radically different in Cuba. The imprint of the idea of the new person in the world beyond Cuba's borders was vast as well. Others saw Cubans debating about policies and institutions that could radically transform four hundred years of capitalist exploitation and individualist political culture.

Further, the Cuban revolution was a metaphor for the drive to end the long history of non-Western societies' dependence upon the colonial and neo-colonial powers. While Che was an exemplar of revolutionary altruism for young people in the rich countries, the movement he was part of suggested that numerically and technologically inferior peoples with the will could defeat those

nations that had oppressed them for centuries. Not only was the
Cuban revolution a symbol of the weak inheriting the earth, it
was also an inspiration for those who had successfully seized
power or had achieved formal power with the end of colonialism.
The Cuban revolution represented the throwing out of old economic models (for a time even the traditional Soviet model), old
ideas on how to organize production, and old notions about the
purposes for which governments exist. Whether in success or
failure, revolutionary governments existed to serve the people.

The Cuban revolution before seizing power *and* afterwards
represented to Third World peoples an example of how to liberate themselves.

Finally, the Cuban revolution (even until this day) has constituted a living experiment that most progressive forces around the
world identify with. Even though each society has its own history,
class structure, level of development, and revolutionary potential,
Cuba's desire to create a government to serve its people and at
the same time to transform them from a traditional consciousness to a revolutionary consciousness is shared by progressives
everywhere. For progressives, Cuba is a laboratory, a grand social
experiment that will provide knowledge for others as they seek
fundamental change in their own societies. If this experiment is
extinguished in the 1990s, given the radical changes in the international system, the history of progressive movements will be set
back dramatically. To this extent, Cuba's successes in the years
ahead are successes of all progressive forces and, similarly, Cuba's
defeats are defeats for all who wish to create egalitarian and
humane societies.

Chapter 2

Themes in Cuban History

Introduction

To understand the driving forces in Cuban political, economic, and cultural life, it is important to reflect on Cuba's history, concentrating on those *shaping experiences* that have set the parameters in which Cubans act today. Several studies have examined in depth the history of the island, detailing historical events, actors, conflicts, and forms of cooperation.[1] Some scholars, enveloped in the details, do not highlight what is called here "shaping experiences." The materials below describe ten such experiences drawn both from the historical scholarship *and* deductions from discourse with contemporary Cubans. The latter source of ideas is critical in that it assumes that the impact of historical experiences derive in large part from the perceptions of contemporary actors in the political process.

Spanish Conquest

The Spanish conquered Cuba between 1511 and 1515 and thus began the process of extermination of the indigenous population such that tribal groups were virtually extinct by the eighteenth century. Those indigenous peoples who survived the initial onslaught found themselves bound to slavery on Spanish landholdings. However, a central feature of Cuban history—revolutionary ferment—began as the early Indian populations fought against the Spanish when it became clear that their goal was conquest.

Central to the institutionalization of Spanish colonialism was
the establishment of private property, which clashed with the
communal forms of land tenure characteristic of the Indian peoples on the island. The Spanish crown allocated lands to Spanish
occupiers and established the policy of assigning indigenous peoples as laborers in designated areas. Disease, repression, suicide,
deadly work in mines and agricultural plantations led to the final
demise of the Indian population as the Spanish consolidated
their control of the island. Consequently, modern Cuba was born
out of conquest, genocidal violence, and a policy of extermination of the indigenous population, a historical fact not lost on the
Cuban people.

Cuba as Sugar Producer

Initially the Spanish sought gold from Cuba and then began to
promote agricultural production. Spain's economic vision was directed at North and Central America when it arrived in the Western Hemisphere but by the eighteenth century, with declining
sugar production elsewhere in the hemisphere, Cuba became a
site for major production, particularly with declining production
and revolution in the French Caribbean colonies.

The demand for sugar increased in the nineteenth century
such that it has become the main prop of the Cuban economy
ever since. Bray and Harding point out that Great Britain's penetration of Cuban markets and trade patterns in the 1760s led to
the spread of Cuban sugar to Northern Europe and North America.[2] While Spanish control of the Cuban sugar economy would
prevail until the 1880s, first the British presence and then that of
the United States led finally to the decline of Spanish control of
the island's economy and its replacement by U.S. domination of
Cuban production and distribution of sugar.

Cuba as Slave Society

Inextricably bound to the emergence of the sugar economy in
Cuba was the establishment of slavery on the island. With the
demise of the indigenous work force as slave labor and the rise of
sugar as the primary commodity, the Spanish imported large
numbers of Africans to provide a new slave labor force on the
sugar plantations. The rising population of Africans was directly

correlated with the increased demand for sugar on the world market and the parallel growth of its production.

The importation of large numbers of African slaves began in the seventeenth century and continued until the end of slavery in Cuba in the 1880s. By 1827 more than 40 percent of the population of Cuba was slave, declining to 36 percent in 1846 and 28 percent in 1862. The decline in the percentage of the population in slavery was due in part to laws that allowed slaves to buy their freedom. Consequently a large non-slave African population emerged in the nineteenth century. In 1827, peoples of African birth constituted over fifty percent of the population.[3]

Because of the pervasiveness of slavery over three hundred years Cuba became a multi-racial and racist society. Racism continued in twentieth century Cuba and served as a vehicle for Cuban rulers to divide the working population. Consequently, the revolution had to come to grips with a history of racial oppression born of the longest experience with slavery in the Western Hemisphere.

Economic Penetration by Great Britain

The Seven Years' War (1756-1763) resulted in Spain's entrance on the side of France against England. Consequently, the Caribbean became a battleground which led to the temporary occupation of Havana by Great Britain in 1762. The occupation led to commerce with North America and Northern Europe breaking the Spanish mercantilist hold on Cuba. While the British occupation was short-lived, Cuban creoles gained a taste of the advantages of commerce with traders outside the mother country. Given Spain's relatively backward economy, the Cuban commercial class could purchase cheaper goods from Great Britain and North America than the obligatory purchases of more expensive and lesser quality goods from Spain. From this point on, the emerging Cuban bourgeoisie sought greater economic independence from Spain.

Also Bray and Harding suggest, with the penetration of the Cuban economy, sugar sales began to shift from Spain to North America, leading by the twentieth century to the rise of dependency on the U.S. economy. This shift was endorsed by the Cuban planter class which sought liberation from the yoke of Spanish control.[4]

What began as commerce between Cuban exporters and im-
porters and merchants from North America and Europe was
transformed over the next two hundred years to the substantial
penetration of foreign capital in Cuba itself, thus displacing Cuban capital. From the eighteenth century to 1959, the Cuban
economy shifted from Spanish control to British and then U.S.
control.

The United States Envisions Control of Cuba

Thomas Jefferson and other early United States leaders
warned that if Spain were not to continue its control of Cuba
then no other power but the United States should dominate the
island. Cuban independence from any outside power would be a
threat to the interests of the United States, particularly the southern United States. Slave revolts such as in Haiti undermined the
legitimacy and security of the slave system in the United States.
Martin Van Buren warned in 1829: "Other considerations con-
nected with a certain class of our population, make it the interest
of the southern section of the Union that no attempt should be
made in that island to throw off the yoke of Spanish dependence,
the first effect of which would be the sudden emancipation of a
numerous slave population, the result of which could not but be
very sensibly felt upon the adjacent shores of the United States."[5]

Further, the Monroe Doctrine conceptualized European penetration of the Western Hemisphere as a challenge to the United
States. While an empty threat at the time of its promulgation, the
Monroe Doctrine proclaimed to the world that the Western
Hemisphere was within the U.S. sphere of influence, to be pro-
tected from outside encroachment. This became an unchallenged
principle repeatedly asserted by U.S. politicians whenever policies
toward Latin American and the Caribbean were discussed.

The North American vision of a Cuba, either bound to Spain,
or, if not possible, tied to the United States dominated thinking
on the Caribbean from the early nineteenth century. This vision
was often justified by the racist assumption that without Spanish
control, or eventually U.S. domination, the island would be un-
governable. The Cubans, indeed, all Latin Americans, were inca-
pable of directing their own affairs and it was one of the burdens
of the United States to insure the stability and economic progress

of the entire region. Consequently, any rebellions against Spanish authority on the island or U.S. advisers after 1898 were contrary to the interests of the United States, and it was thought, the Cuban people.

Revolutionary Ferment

Because of its history, Cuba has been a society in revolt ever since the encroachment of the Spanish. Indians fought against their conquest and rebelled against the slave labor and expropriation of land they experienced under Spanish rule. African slaves revolted episodically, sometimes after developing organizations and plans to overthrow Spanish colonial and creole oppression. Indigenous land owners, the creoles, revolted in support of political and economic freedom from foreign domination, particularly against the heavy hand of Spanish mercantilism. And, in the nineteenth and twentieth centuries peasants, workers, Afro-Cubans, students, and nationalists rose up against the Spanish, against the United States occupiers, and against Cuban rulers who acted in collaboration with foreign economic and political interests.

The Cuban revolution of 1959 was inspired by the failed revolution of 1868 and the successful struggle against Spanish colonialism in the 1890s. The father of revolutionary Cuba, from the perspective of contemporary Cubans, is José Martí, the poet, educator, and political leader who organized the movement in the 1890s that led, after his death, to the victory of the Cuban people over the Spanish overlords, only to have their victory taken away by the United States.

In the period from the mid-1920s until 1933, modern revolutionary ideas and parties formed as Cubans of many classes and occupations organized to force dictator Gerardo Machado from office, a feat that was achieved in 1933.

To circumvent a more radical outcome, a Cuban army sergeant named Fulgencio Batista surfaced, with U.S. support, to govern Cuba. He ruled directly from 1933 until 1944 and returned to power via a coup in 1952. His last period in power was marked by particularly brutal rule. The response of the Cuban people to Batista's repression escalated to the latest phase in the revolutionary process.

Central to any understanding of Cuban political life is this revolutionary tradition, endorsed pridefully by the people and referred to often by Cuba's leaders. Perhaps the fundamental animating vision of this revolutionary ferment spanning five hundred years has been a spirit of nationalism and a deep passion for self-determination. This pride in nationhood and insistence on the right to determine its own destiny is at the heart of Cuba's contemporary struggle to survive the radical changes in the current international system.

Nineteenth Century United States Penetration

Given the vision of its leaders and the post-Civil War growth in the U.S. economy, U.S. foreign investors established a substantial presence in the Cuban economy by the 1880s. U.S. capital entered Cuba to build modern sugar mills and in the process forced smaller Cuban sugar operations into decline. Further, Spanish entrepreneurs were eclipsed by the newer U.S. capital. In many cases, local planters were integrated into the larger U.S. operations. The power of the U.S. economic role on the island was further highlighted by the fact that 82 percent of Cuba's sugar was shipped to the United States by 1880.[6]

During the last decade of the nineteenth century, depression hit the U.S. economy and Spanish/U.S. tariff concessions involving trade with Cuba ended. There were pressures from U.S. business people to seek new markets for U.S. goods. Naval strategist Admiral Alfred Mahan linked successful commerce with the need for a navy to protect trade routes. Economic penetration and a naval presence coincided with direct political control of trading partners, he claimed. This was particularly true in the case of the Caribbean which he, like so many others, viewed as the property of the United States.

The penetration of the Cuban economy, the rising spirit of jingoism in the United States, the revolutionary ferment in Cuba, and the emergence of the United States as a global power all stimulated the drive toward war. The United States intervened in the war between Cuba and Spain and positioned itself so that it could circumvent the coming to power of the victorious Cuban revolutionaries.

The United States Controls Cuba From 1898 to 1959

Next to the conquest itself U.S. hegemonic control over Cuba has been the most significant shaping experience in the island's history. The McKinley Administration intervened in Cuba during what became known as the Spanish-American War and after speedy military victory established its presence and control of the island's affairs. In fact, the peace treaty signed by the U.S. and the Spanish occurred without the presence of any Cuban leaders. A Cuban provisional government was ignored by the occupying power as U.S. military officers ruled Cuba until 1902.

The relationship between Cuba and the United States is best symbolized by the Platt Amendment, an amendment to legislation in the U.S. Senate that prescribed what the U.S. role in Cuba should be. This amendment became part of the Cuban constitution. The provisions of the Platt Amendment included the right to establish a permanent military base on the island (Guantanamo Base still exists). The amendment gave the United States the right to intervene militarily when U.S. interests were threatened on the island. Also the amendment gave the United States the right to pass judgment on Cuban treaties and loans. In sum, by unilateral declaration, the United States proclaimed its right to rule the affairs of Cuba if and when it chose.[7]

After 1902 when Cuba allegedly established an independent government, U.S. capital poured in. By 1905 U.S. citizens owned one-fourth of Cuba's territory. Between 1902 and 1922, Americans built 27 new sugar mills processing one-half of Cuba's sugar. By 1926, seven U.S. companies owned one-half of all Cuban sugar. As Cuban sugar flowed to the U.S., U.S. goods made their way to the island. Further, consumer patterns, schools, textbooks were all dominated by the United States.[8]

When revolutionary ferment threatened disruption of the island's economic and political life, U.S. marines would be sent to reestablish order or diplomats would participate with local Cubans to ease from office the targets of disenchantment. The U.S. worked with Batista to overthrow the dreaded dictator Gerardo Machado in 1933. After Machado was defeated, the United States aided Batista in carrying out a coup replacing reformer Ramon Grau San Martin with Batista himself. The U.S. remained loyal to Batista when he was in power from 1933 to 1944 and 1952 to 1958.

As the twentieth century unfolded U.S. citizens controlled more and more of Cuba's economy. By 1960 U.S. companies had investments totaling $1.5 billion in sugar mills, mines, and large manufacturing plants. U.S. investors controlled 80 percent of Cuba's public utilities, 90 percent of its mines, 90 percent of its cattle ranches, 50 percent of its railways, 40 percent of its sugar, 100 percent of its oil refineries, and controlled 25 percent of bank deposits in Cuba.[9] Most of the profits derived from these investments were repatriated abroad so that little Cuban benefit was gained from the foreign investment. Obviously Cuba exercised little control of its own economy.

The inextricable bond between the economics and politics of hegemony is suggested by Bray and Harding:

> Economic development would have required monetary autonomy, the power to modify payment on Cuba's international debt, national control over foreign commerce, national planning, and a radical redistribution of income. However, U.S. business interests required political stability, full payments on loans, laissez faire in commerce and fiscal policy, and the predominance of foreign private and international banks. Given the basic acceptance of U.S. domination, both by Batista and the Cuban bourgeoisie, there could be no economic development, nor would Batista allow the political expression of nationalism."[10]

Cuban economics and politics were dominated by the United States. As Bray and Harding suggest, "the political expression of nationalism," the drive for autonomy, for a Cuban way of life was squelched by the institutionalized relationship between Cuba and the United States symbolized by the Platt Amendment. A 400-year history of a people thirsting for independence and self-determination, and manifested in an ideology of nationalism confronted an economic, political, and military force whose goal was to prohibit it. Reflecting on this confrontation of opposites, the Cuban/U.S. cold and hot wars of the 1960s, 1970s, and 1980s seem inevitable.

A Weak Indigenous Bourgeoisie

The history of colonialism and neo-colonialism was marked by the institutionalization of economic and political dependency, first on Spain, then on the United States. The long-term effect of dependency was the diminution in the development of indigenous political and economic institutions and leaders able to plant their own character on even those foreign made institutions.

Concretely, since the sugar economy was so dominated by Spanish and U.S. investors and their governments, there did not develop in Cuba an indigenous bourgeoisie able to control at least a partial share of the Cuban economy. Periodically, when Cuban entrepreneurs rose up in opposition to Spanish mercantilism, they were crushed, thus reducing the size and power of the Cuban upper classes. With the massive U.S. presence in the sugar industry from the 1880s, there was little opportunity for Cubans to own or control this key sector of the economy.

One significant byproduct of a weakened bourgeoisie was that Cubans favored by the dominating power gained material rewards in politics rather than economics. In the twentieth century some Cubans gained wealth and power by corruption in conjunction with the state. Politics was the vehicle for upward mobility, which created a Cuban political life that bore little relationship to the needs of the people nor to their sense of nationalism. The mythology around such figures as Fidel Castro and Che Guevara, self-sacrificing persons willing to give their lives for "the people," radically contradicted the notion Cubans had of their political leaders.

The Cuban state in the twentieth century, because of lack of identification with the needs of a growing bourgeoisie, was particularly influenced by powerful interests, usually foreign, although occasionally Cuban leaders such as Batista would respond to demands from dispossessed groups like labor to mollify them. The end result was that the state and Cuban politicians served at the discretion of and were supported by foreign interests, particularly from the United States.

Great Wealth for the Few:
Immiseration for the Many

Commentators on Cuban economic life before the revolution have pointed out that Cuba was one of the more developed Latin American societies yet there was enormous poverty, especially in the rural areas. In 1956 one-half of the Cuban people lived in rural areas where the per capita income was $100. In 1959 600,000 people were unemployed, one-half lived without electricity, 64 percent had no running water, 3.5 million people lived in

slums, and rents constituted 1/3 of incomes. Forty percent of
Cuba's population was illiterate and 150,000 people had tubercu-
losis. Less than two percent of the landowners owned 46 percent
of the land.[11]

Therefore, the economic profile of Cuba at the time of the
revolution was that of a country with predominant resources
owned and controlled by foreign investors, a small wealthy Cuban upperclass, often enriched by government service and politics, and a large peasant and working class population that was
desperately poor, with limited access to medical care and education. This was coupled with a political system that resisted all
demands for change and, as ferment grew in the 1950s, became
violently repressive.

**Multi-story mural of Che Guevara faces the Plaza
of the Revolution.**

Chapter 3

Three Views of the Cuban Revolution: 1960

Introduction

From the time that the rebel army of the 26th of July Movement marched into Havana in January, 1959, the Cuban revolution has had a fascination for peoples all over the world. This is particularly the case for progressive peoples whose politics are driven by visions of alternative forms of social, political, and economic organization to better satisfy human needs.

The energy, commitment, brashness, and experimentalism of the young Cuban revolution served as a magnet drawing scholars, journalists, and political activists to the island to see for themselves what was happening. Four such persons visited Cuba in 1960 and wrote, in three volumes, of what they saw. Their texts analyzed the history of Cuba, offered explanations of the underlying dynamics of Cuban society, and offered predictions of the future of the revolution and its consequences for peoples around the world.

Thirty-one years later, Cuba faces a new set of circumstances internationally and new, and perhaps more dangerous, threats to its revolution. By returning to these 1960 texts, those interested in Cuba may gain insights about what drove the revolutionary process then and what, perhaps, of that set of forces still bears on the Cuban revolution in 1992. How much of the visions, the threats to survival, the economics, the politics, the culture have changed and how much has stayed the same? It is suggested here that Leo Huberman and Paul Sweezy's, *Cuba: Anatomy of a Revolu-*

tion, Joseph North's, *Cuba: Hope of a Hemisphere* and C. Wright Mills' *Listen Yankee,* provided insights about Cuba in 1960 that are still relevant today.[1]

Leo Huberman and Paul Sweezy Describe A Revolution in Process

These authors begin their Preface with a description of their methodology—that is, a combination of journalism and scholarship. Journalism implies speed and scholarship careful deliberation. The combination of the two, they said, offers the most expeditious way of analyzing "one of the most original and important social transformations of our time."[2] Their work drew upon existent scholarship on Cuba, a reading of Cuban history, and an analysis of the Cuba they observed in two visits, one in March, 1960 and the other in September and October, 1960. (In fact all three books under consideration here combine journalism and scholarship and serve as models for this writing.)

Huberman and Sweezy divide their text into three parts: the background of the revolution, the making of the revolution, and the revolution in power. In the first section, the authors succinctly describe Cuba's history, its political economy, the sources of its wealth and power, and the system of stratification that led to opulence on one pole and poverty on the other.

They point to the contradiction between the natural wealth of the island as to climate, arable land and location, the relatively high level of development of Cuba compared with other Third World countries, and the devastating poverty that characterized the life of the Cuban people, particularly in rural areas. In the 1950s less than half the population of the island had access to water, basic sanitation, and electricity. Health care was scarce and educational facilities limited. Unemployment constituted 25 percent of the population.[3]

For these authors the historic source of the immiseration of the Cuban people was sugar. Sugar plantations were owned by a small number of wealthy Cuban landlords coupled with the increasing control by United States investors. During each economic crisis, when international demand for sugar declined, indigenous sugar entrepreneurs would be forced to liquidate their holdings. U.S. investors at each juncture, the 1880s, 1900s, 1920s, and 1950s, gained a greater control of Cuba's sugar crop and processing facilities. "In 1896, ten percent of Cuba's total production of sugar came from American owned mills; in 1914, thirty-five percent; in 1926 sixty-three percent."[4] By the 1950s, the United States literally controlled the Cuban economy.

Since the island's economic activity was largely devoted to sugar production, Cuba had to purchase foodstuffs and manufactured goods. Those who owned the sugar plantations and processing plants earned healthy profits while workers in the fields and the factories lived on meager wages. For the bulk of plantation workers, work existed largely during the harvest season—four months of the year. Workers spent much of the rest of the time unemployed. The authors quote with approval Jose Marti's 1883 admonition against single crop economies: "A people commits suicide the day on which it bases its existence on a single crop."[5]

Huberman and Sweezy discussed the process of making the revolution and the ideas behind the 26 of July Movement which led the assault against the Batista dictatorship. Central to the success of the revolution was the appeal to the peasantry, the class most victimized by the Batista dictatorship, the one-crop economy, and foreign domination. For the authors the central thrust of the revolution was the goal of improving the living conditions for the vast majority of Cubans.

This "rational humanist" vision was reflected, they said, in Fidel Castro's famous courtroom speech called "History Will Absolve Me." This speech, a discourse on Cuban history and the needs of the Cuban people, was made before a court in Santiago de Cuba before Castro was sentenced to jail after the failed coup attempt in 1953. In the speech, Castro referred to those for whom a revolution is to be made "the vast unredeemed masses, to whom all make promises and whom all deceive."[6]

He then disaggregated the concept of the masses and by so doing illustrated his vision of revolutionary change. He spoke of 700,000 unemployed Cubans and 500,000 farm laborers who worked only four months a year and lived in hovels with no land for personal cultivation. He talked of 400,000 industrial laborers and stevedores who had their retirement funds embezzled by bosses and politicians, 100,000 small farmers working on small parcels of rented land, teachers and other professionals who could not find attractive work, and small business persons weighed down with debts. For all these strata Cuba faced six problems: "The problems concerning land, the problem of industrialization, the problem of housing, the problem of unemployment, the problem of education, and the problem of the health of the people; these are the six problems we would take immediate steps to resolve, along with the restoration of public liberties and political democracy." [7]

Castro elaborated in detail on the depths of each of these problems and offered a platform for their solution. A revolutionary government would establish a maximal amount of land that each kind of enterprise could own. A new government would give landless peasants land and would encourage the formation of agricultural cooperatives. Technical assistance, equipment, and other needs would be provided to small peasant farmers and agricultural cooperatives. Rents would be cut in half, hovels would be torn down and replaced with multiple-dwelling units. Electricity would be provided all across the island. With the redistribution of land and the dramatic increase in housing construction, the problem of unemployment would be eliminated. Finally, Castro said, the government would devote its resources to education reform.

For those who would question the feasibility of these projects, Castro claimed;

> Cuba could easily provide for a population three times as great as it now has, so there is no excuse for the abject poverty of a single one of its present inhabitants. The markets should be overflowing with produce, pantries should be full, all hands should be working. This is not an inconceivable thought. What is inconceivable is that anyone should go to bed hungry, that children should die for lack of medical attention; what is inconceivable is that 30 percent of our farm people cannot write their names and 99 percent of them know nothing of Cuba's history. What is inconceivable is that the majority of our rural people are now living in worse circumstances than were the Indians Columbus discovered living in the fairest land that human eyes had ever seen. [8]

Castro then argued that when tyrannies violated the principles of constitutional government, in this case the Cuban Constitution, the people had the right to rebel to reestablish legitimate government that was based upon the social contract between rulers and ruled. Therefore, while the court before whom he was speaking would sentence him, "history will absolve me."

Although sentenced to 15 years in prison, Castro was released in 1955 by Batista with the hope that out of prison Castro would be demythologized. Batista also felt that by releasing Castro, support for his government would increase. Shortly after his release Castro departed for Mexico City where he began planning for the rebellion to take place.

Castro and a small coterie of revolutionaries sailed for Cuba from Mexico in December 1956, and thus began the saga of the revolutionary war that led to the fall of Batista in 1959. Huberman and Sweezy emphasized the passive, then active support of the peasantry as the bulwark of the tiny revolutionary army. Peasants in the Sierra Maestra mountains where the revolutionaries established camps were the beneficiaries of land reform, schooling, and health care administered by the rebels. These concrete acts convinced peasants that this revolutionary movement did represent their interests and word of this spread throughout the country. Because of the level of support given the revolutionaries by the peasants, the rebel armies were able to defeat a government force that probably was twenty times larger, with modern military equipment provided by the United States.

The support of the peasantry, the authors suggested, constituted the most fundamental fact of the revolution; the U.S. support of the repressive Batista government the second most important fact. With a peasant base in the countryside and anger at the United States, revolutionary fervor spread to workers, students, middle class professionals and business people and others, thus consolidating a multi-class mass movement whose goals included democratic change and fundamental social and economic change. Of course, some supporters of the 26th of July movement supported only the first goal while others supported both.

Huberman and Sweezy concluded their discussion of the guerrilla war period by reflecting on the role of U.S. media coverage of the events in Cuba. To the authors, media accounts inaccurately reported the course of the revolution, always underestimating its level of support and prospects of success. After Batista's armies were defeated and the new government in place, the media portrayed public trials of Batista officers as barbaric, since some were sentenced to death. The authors indicated that such stories should have been placed in some historical context: the crimes that the officers engaged in and the demands of the population for retribution well beyond the bounds of justice.

The authors concluded that the treatment of prisoners was humane which they claimed was a reflection of the fundamental character of the revolutionary movement:

> Their treatment of army prisoners during the war had already proved that Fidel Castro and the other rebel leaders were humanitarians—not the bloodthirsty monsters they were depicted in press and radio following the trials. In fact, it was their very humanity which made them revolutionists in the first place. And it was their very humanity which dictated the program they instituted after their conquest of power—a program designed to alleviate the misery of their less fortunate countrymen.[9]

In their discussion of "the revolution in power" Huberman and Sweezy emphasized again the rural character of the revolution and the symbiotic relationship between the leader of the revolution, Fidel Castro, peasants and agricultural workers. Emphasizing the class character of the revolution in struggle and power, the authors indicated that three quarters of those Cubans employed in agriculture were agricultural laborers, only about 11 percent ranchers and farmers. Collectively 40 percent of the work force was in agriculture. About three percent of the workforce consisted of industrial workers in the countryside, workers in the sugar mills. The interaction between the agricultural workers and the industrial workers in the mills constituted a working class base of support for the revolution.[10]

Upon the defeat of Batista a new government was established drawing representation, not only from the revolutionaries, but the middle and upper class opponents of Batista. As Huberman and Sweezy labeled it, their existed a dual system of government; one set of personnel supportive of modest reforms in the political process but opposed to fundamental social and economic change and the other set of personnel linked to the 26th of July Movement committed to political change and social and economic change. For this latter group the ranked priorities of change would privilege the social and economic changes, as reflected in the "History Will Absolve Me" speech.

It was not too long before the coalition between the two factions was rent asunder. The most fundamental stimulus for the breakdown of consensus was the Agrarian Reform Law of May, 1959 that expropriated large landholdings from wealthy Cubans and foreigners. It is at this point that the counterrevolution started. Cubans and U.S. policymakers initiated the crusade against the government, in which Castro's forces were consolidating control, under the banner of anti-communism. In rebuttal, the new government labeled those waving the anti-communist banner as counterrevolutionaries.

Huberman and Sweezy argued that the revolution was always radical in that it was motivated both by the vision of political change and the necessities of social and economic change. The fulfillment of the basic needs of the population at large required nationalizations, planning, expropriations, and the privileging of poor and rural peoples in public policy. These acts conflicted with the material interests of wealthy Cubans and foreign investors. Real revolution and violent opposition to it was almost inevitable.

While inevitable, the shaping vision and language of the revolution was not labeled by the revolutionaries. Leaders like Castro referred to their revolution as pursuing a different path than capitalism or communism. In fact, governmental officials and sympathetic foreign observers such as Jean-Paul Sartre characterized the revolution as pragmatic in that its character was a result of the totality of individual policies of reform and as to policy was the result of an amalgam of the values of liberalism and Marxism.

However, for Huberman and Sweezy, "the rational humanism" of the Cuban revolution led logically to the establishment of a socialist economy. The public sector would continue to grow, they predicted, and the private sector would become more marginalized as the state, largely reflected in the initiatives of the Institute for Agrarian Reform and the rebel army, would assume more of the burdens in establishing new health care and educational systems, a diversified economy, adequate housing, and a better life for the people. Ironically, they suggested, the Cuban revolution will have been the only socialist revolution made by non-communists in the twentieth century. The Cuban Communist Party was supportive of the revolution because they largely agreed with its goals but their role in its evolution was exceedingly modest. The leaders of the revolution in power remained the leaders of the 26th of July movement.

Irrespective of whether the Cuban revolution was a "communist" one or not, the authors expected increased attacks upon it, particularly from the United States. The memory of the U.S. supported military ouster of Jacob Arbenz from power in Guatemala was still fresh in the minds of political activists and analysts alike. However, the Cuban revolutionary government had the one significant difference as compared with Guatemala; the Cuban army was the rebel army. In Guatemala, the army was independent of the Arbenz government and hence subject to pressures from the United States, which led it to withdraw its support from Arbenz.

Mindful of U.S. efforts to control the hemisphere's nations, the authors discussed political, economic, and military means the United States and anti-Castro Cubans might use to overturn the revolution. The authors felt that the existence of a Socialist Bloc and a powerful Soviet Union increased the freedom of maneuver of the Cuban government, that could help the Cubans overcome economic dependence on the United States. Because of its salience in later chapters, it is important to quote from the authors on this point:

> The truth is that Soviet trade and aid, far from enslaving Cuba, is enabling her for the first time in her history to achieve a measure of genuine independence from all foreign powers. Since the time of Martí, this has been the fervent desire of every Cuban patriot. That it is now being realized in practice is surely one of the greatest achievements of the Revolution. And it is an achievement which will be treasured and fought for through thick and thin by the vast majority of the Cuban people.[11]

In an epilogue written after a return visit to Cuba in September 1960, the authors described the scenario of escalating tensions between Cuba and the United States, including the ending of purchases of Cuban sugar and the full embargo of trade with Cuba. Also they wrote that counterrevolutionaries within Cuba were relatively unpopular and were divided. They asked under what circumstances the counterrevolutionaries would pose a serious threat to the regime. Their answer was relevant to 1960 and as discussed in later chapters may be relevant in 1992:

The answer to these questions is clearly to be sought in the economic sphere. If the economic development programs of the regime succeed, there is no reason to doubt that its popular support will be maintained and the counter-revolutionaries will continue to be frustrated. If on the other hand there are serious failures in the economic sphere, the opposition will grow and the enthusiasm of the regime's supporters will flag. Under such conditions, the threat of counter-revolution would become very real indeed. The fate of the Cuban Revolution, in other words, is crucially dependent on its economic success or failure.[12]

After reporting the strengths in the agricultural programs and the problems with the drive toward industrialization, Huberman and Sweezy suggested that if the United States left Cuba alone, the revolution would surely survive. Inadequacies of personnel and organization would be solved in the years ahead. With outside assistance, the authors expected major gains toward the liquidation of the host of problems that were articulated by Castro in his famous courtroom speech. Counterrevolutionaries would lose hope and their ranks dwindle. "Cuba, in short, could become a showplace of socialism and a model for other underdeveloped countries to emulate."[13]

However, the United States would not leave Cuba alone. In fact, they reported on the training and mobilization that would reach fruition as the Bay of Pigs invasion nine months after their visit. Despite these efforts and the enormous power of the United States, it could not impose its will on the Cuban people, particularly as the constellation of forces in the world was tilting away from the U.S. And the epilogue's opening statement, an extract from a 1960 statement by Che Guevara, described the fundamental interconnection between the path that Cuba would take in the future and the policies of the United States.

What lies ahead depends greatly on the United States. With the exception of our agrarian reform, which the people of Cuba desired and initiated themselves, all of our radical measures have been a direct response to direct aggressions by powerful monopolists, of which your country is the chief exponent. U.S. pressure on Cuba has made necessary the 'radicalization' of the revolution. To know how much further Cuba will go, it will be easier to ask the U..S. government how far it plans to go.[14]

Joseph North Analyzes a National and Democratic Revolution

Joseph North, one-time editor of the *New Masses*, visited Cuba in January, 1959 shortly after the revolutionary armies moved into Havana as the combat drew to a close. North returned in the spring of 1960. He indicated in the Foreword to his volume that it was written to help forestall a U.S. military assault on the island nation. At the point of writing, 1,500 marines had landed at Guantanamo, the U.S. military installation on the island.

For the revolutionary regime, the troop movements suggested a possible U.S. military attack on Cuba. North reminded readers what he said all Latin Americans were reflecting upon, that is the U.S.-stimulated military assault on the reform government of Jacob Arbenz in Guatemala in 1954. The United States government by 1960 was trying to destabilize and overthrow the Castro government as it had the Arbenz government.

The author indicated that upon return from his second trip to Cuba, he was called to testify before the Senate Internal Security Committee and questioned about his Cuban trips and writings. The goal of this effort, he claimed, was to intimidate those who might be interested in visiting Cuba and seeing the progress of the revolution for themselves.

North wrote that while the goal of U.S. policy toward Cuba is the same as that of U.S. policy toward Guatemala, the historical conditions had changed since 1954 and consequently the goal would be very difficult to achieve. The majority of humankind supports Cuba, he said, and many peoples had the resources in 1961 to support Cuba materially. Consequently, it would be most rational for the United States to establish policies toward Cuba that reduce tensions and reestablish trade and diplomatic relations.

North, as with the other authors examined in this chapter, discussed the legacy of Cuban history. Most importantly, North made it clear that the Cuban revolution and the new regime was the latest phase of the 400-year struggle of the Cuban people to liberate themselves from foreign and domestic domination. "Uprisings, time and again, were crushed; slave revolts were overwhelmed by gun and cannon; the many wars for liberty in the nineteenth century were prelude to this armed landing and the contemporary brave work that had been going on underground since the Dictator Batista had overthrown the republic in 1953 in a palace revolt." [15]

The United States played a significant role in this history because Batista "was aided by big-time American money that regarded him as the best guarantor for their enormous investments and profits—well over a billion dollars in holdings was the stake."[16] North wrote of an interview with Raul Castro in which the U.S. role in Cuban affairs was discussed. Castro's perspective was that the Cuban people would have secured their independence from outside control in the 1890s if the United States had not intervened in the Spanish Cuban war and imposed the Platt Amendment on the Cuban people. As a result Cuba became a "semi-colony of Wall Street," a situation that Raul Castro said would be changed.

North, a long-time member of the U.S. Communist Party, wrote about the role of the Cuban communist party (Partido Socialista Popular) in the revolutionary struggle. He pointed to its significance for the final victory while at the same time developed the view that the Cuban regime was a nationalist and democratic one, not a socialist one.

The PSP newspaper, *Hoy*, had been the second largest newspaper in the country until it was banned when Batista seized power in 1952. The newspaper from that point on was published and circulated underground by party members along with their distribution of large numbers of pamphlets addressing problems experienced by the Cuban people. This dissemination of materials critical of the Cuban government was dangerous, as police terror led to thousands of deaths in the 1950s. Also, North pointed out, many PSP members had participated in the guerrilla struggle against the Batista armies in the Sierra Maestras. Three party members were among the 17 commanders who led the rebel armies by the war's end.

North summarized a discussion he had with Carlos Rafael Rodriguez, then editor of *Hoy*, about the nature of the revolution. It was emphasized that the revolutionaries were a broad coalition of peasants, workers, students, and others. Only the largest landowners and the wealthiest Cubans opposed the revolution. The revolution was not a socialist revolution but "'an advanced, popular national revolution,' for sovereignty, for independence, for the civil rights of the folk."[17]

North characterized the new Cuban regime as *anti-imperialist*,

because it exercises *national sovereignty*, both in domestic as well as
foreign policy, in its own way, not in the way others order it; that it
seeks trade with *all* countries; that it has taken over the oil refineries; that it carries out a radical agrarian reform; that it eliminates
racism; that it promotes cooperatives; that it has converted barracks
into schools, that it is conquering illiteracy.[18]

The United States, he said, was fueling the fears of United
States citizens by labeling Cuba "communist." In fact, Cuba was
not a socialist state although ultimately it would move in that
direction. Confusion was being sown because Cuba has developed a large public sector and as well as organizing the countryside into agricultural cooperatives. "That Cuba nationalized these
vast sectors of its economy, most of which was foreign-owned,
does not mean it is practicing socialism. It means primarily that
the new government recognizes that large private interests, mo-
nopoly capital, are counter-revolutionary and seek to overthrow
the new setup by industrial, political, sabotage and armed upris-
ing or invasion."[19]

As to the structure of the regime, North reported after his first
visit that the broad coalition of leaders included conservatives
who opposed fundamental changes in the class structure. Their
vision of the revolution was one that would displace the dictator
Batista and replace him with a more open political system. Others
in the leadership of the new government were committed to
substantial social change such that the resources of the society are
distributed more equitably.

The agrarian reform laws established in rebel held territories
in the period of struggle and the May, 1959 law illustrated the
vision of many of the rebels of a new society in which people
have access to land, food, health care, education, and housing.
North reported on visits to newly created agricultural cooperatives where workers were engaged in construction of buildings
for housing and public assemblies. Plans were underway for re-
claiming the lands of *latifundists* for the planting of crops for
domestic consumption. He told of a visit to one agricultural cooperative where the resident agronomist waxed eloquently about
the new breed of hardy and tasty tomatoes that was being grown
on the land. Success at producing foods for domestic consumption would end the dependence on foreign sources of supply and

the concentration on sugar production. The Cuban revolutionaries believed that Cuba could be self-sufficient in the production of food for its people.

Many rural dwellers were agricultural workers, part-time sugar cane cutters or sugar mill workers, rather than traditional peasants. Because of their occupational status and the general influence of workers ideas in the countryside, rural peoples seemed eager to join agricultural cooperatives rather than secure the 67 acres of land they were individually entitled to by decree of the new government.

North defended the escalating pattern of expropriations by the Cuban government of foreign-owned corporations, banks, and landholdings as well as those of wealthy Cubans. He said foreign investors, primarily from the United States, had controlled oil refineries, public utilities, the tourist industry, sugar production, and all other significant assets. Profits flowed out of the country so that Cubans did not gain from the basic wealth of their society. An example of the kind of control outsiders had over the Cuban economy was demonstrated by the refusal of U.S. oil companies with refineries in Cuba to refine oil purchased from the Soviet Union. If the refineries had not been expropriated, the Cubans could not purchase the oil from the Soviet Union.

As the new Cuban government began to assert its independence by instituting new laws such as the agrarian reform program and developing trade agreements with the Soviet Union and other non-traditional economic partners, the United States escalated its opposition to the new government. Most significantly, the United States virtually halted all purchases of sugar from Cuba. In the past, the United States purchased sixty to seventy percent of Cuba's sugar. This was soon followed by a full economic embargo of the island.

These moves were taken with the expectation that the new regime would collapse. However, Cuba deepened its ties with the Soviet Union and the countries of Eastern Europe. North's view was that the new Cuban ties with the socialist countries "...helps Cuba to strike out on an independent economic policy, enabling her to deal with any nation to their mutual advantage."[20]

Throughout the text, North illustrated ways in which the U.S. media distorted and misled the citizenry about the Cuban revolution. After the reform laws were instituted and the trade agree-

ments with the Soviet Union completed, the U.S. press reported
events from the island in anti-communist terms, much like that
communicated by the Eisenhower Administration. The media
gave voice to anti-Castro Cubans and U.S. officials who called on
the United States to intervene militarily to oust Castro from
power.

As a result of the U.S. media portrait of Castro as a new
dictator and Cuba a communist dictatorship, U.S. citizens were
ignorant of the broad popularity of the Cuban revolution
throughout Latin America. In fact, the Cuban revolution represented, he said, the future of the Third World. Anti-colonial,
democratic, and independence-minded movements will create
revolutions throughout Latin America, as well as Asia and Africa.
Cuba, then:

> tells all Latin America that freedom, sovereignty, independence,
> and a bettered life for all its inhabitants, is within grasp. One needs
> but the will to challenge the old, the moribund, the dying slave-own-
> ing colonial system. That is what Cuba has said to the world and that
> is why Cuba today is the cause of all decent men the world over.[21]

C. Wright Mills Demands That Yankees Listen to the Cuban Story

C. Wright Mills, the distinguished and controversial sociologist
of the postwar period in the United States, visited Cuba in the fall
of 1960. He wrote that he had not given much thought to the
Cuban revolution until 1960. When he became intrigued with it,
he read all he could about Cuba before and since the revolution.
He then visited the country in August 1960 and, because of the
general familiarity of Cubans with several of his prior writings
such as *The Power Elite*, he was able to secure interviews with a
variety of people. They included many revolutionary leaders and
government spokespersons including Fidel Castro.

As a result of this experience, the author wrote a book that is
supposed to represent a composite Cuban voice addressing a U.S.
audience. C. Wright Mills claimed that while the writing was his,
he was accurately representing the thinking of the many Cubans
he had met. Therefore the text was really the voice of the Cuban
revolution, not his own. To highlight this point the author has a
preface entitled "Note to the Reader, I" and a postscript entitled
"Note to the Reader, II," which are presented as his own voice.

Mills wrote about his approach:

> Most of the words are mine—although not all of them; the arguments, the tone, the interpretations, the tang and feel—they are in the main directly Cuban. I have merely organized them in the most direct and immediate fashion of which I am capable. Here, I am trying to say, is what Cubans in the middle of their revolution are now thinking about that revolution, about its place within their own lives, and about its future. Here is something of their optimism, their exhaustion, their confusion, their anger, their ranting, their worries—and yet, if you listen well, you will catch the reasonable tone which does pervade the revolutionary argument when it is discussed seriously and in private.[22]

With this explanation as a starting point, the collective voice of the Cuban revolution discusses a variety of subjects, directly addressing the U.S. reader. These include discussions of Cuba as representative of Third World experience, the Cuban revolution as continuation of the struggle for liberation and at the same time a new beginning, conditions that breed revolution, U.S.-Cuban relations and U.S. imperialism, the emerging close relationship between Cuba and the Socialist countries, and the need for a new United States foreign policy toward Cuba and the Third World in general.

Mills argued, or rather his Cuban sources argued, that the countries of Asia, Africa, and Latin America constituted "a hungry bloc," all experiencing colonial or neo-colonial pasts that left their peoples poor and powerless. In this regard, then, Cuba was not different from other countries. Revolutionary ferment in Cuba was very much the byproduct of the same kind of economic and political factors that were stimulating revolutions all across the globe. "In Africa, in Asia, as well as in Latin America, the people behind this voice are becoming strong in a kind of fury they've never known before. As nations, they are young: to them the world is new."[23] Or later: "Today, the revolution is going on in Cuba. Tomorrow—not next year—it is going to be going on elsewhere." [24]

Hunger, low life expectancies, illiteracy, and a number of other byproducts of poverty characterize the vast majority of the world's population, which constitutes the major common experience of most nations and peoples. Further, Mills' revolutionary claimed, many of the nations of the "Communist bloc" were

formerly part of the hungry bloc but no longer are. Consequently, the Socialist countries seem attractive to poor peoples
seeking radical change. Communist countries "are coming out of
hunger" whereas in many countries still capitalist "we don't see
that kind of development."[25]

Addressing the Cuban revolution more directly, the composite
voice described the economic and political conditions in Cuba
before the revolution. First, Havana was a city that had been
engulfed in sin, corruption, greed, prostitution, gambling and
poverty. In 1957 there were 270 brothels and over 700 bars, and
thousands of slot machines were placed throughout the island.

Seven hundred thousand Cubans were unemployed when the
revolutionaries came to power. On average, 25 percent of workers and peasants were unemployed. Nine out of ten rural dwellings (bohios) had only kerosene lighting, less than 3 percent had
indoor plumbing. More than half the dwellings did not even have
outdoor privies. Two-thirds of the rural children did not attend
elementary school and most of those who began school dropped
out by the eighth grade. Vividly Mills' revolutionary pointed out
that "Yankee, in case you've forgotten, or if you never knew,
poverty is dreary. It is a way of dying yet not dying. Poverty
means no shoes, and the rich, fat worms crawling in the intestines
of your children, up through the naked soles of their feet. Poverty in Cuba meant eight people existing—who could say living?—in a miserable, filthy shack, with a floor of dirt, a leaking
roof of thatch, and open fires to cook on, huddling around,
coughing in the smoke." In sum "That old order is an order of
police terror and grief and poverty and disease and illiteracy and
the corrupted politics of the thief and the capitalism of the rob-
ber..."[27]

Given the squalid lives of the old order and the political system that supported it, the Cuban revolution constituted "a new
beginning." This new beginning entailed the establishment of a
Cuban economic and political system that would experiment with
new structures and policies to radically transform the lives of the
Cuban people. This experiment may in fact constitute a new
beginning for the Americas as well.

Revolution was a process whereby reality itself was redefined
and subsequently changed. Revolution was a phenomena in
which fantasy and reality were fused in a "great moment of

truth."[28] Concretely, the existence of poverty meant that there was a need for economic construction; the existence of ignorance, a need for education; and external threat, the need for a citizen's militia. "It is not so much that we are rebuilding Cuban society, for there was nothing here of much worth to rebuild. We are building a new society, from top to bottom, and in all spheres of our lives. It is the birth of a nation we are living through."[29]

The revolutionaries in *Listen, Yankee* described the historical context for the political repression and economic exploitation experienced by Cubans. Economically, the island was consigned to a one-crop sugar economy in the era of Spanish colonialism and reinforced after independence by U.S. investors. Since the 1840s, U.S. policymakers defined Cuba as fundamentally a part of the United States, from the Ostend Manifesto in the 1840s (a unilateral declaration by politicians that Cuba belonged to the U.S.), to the Platt Amendment, to military support for Batista.

The driving force for U.S. policy toward Cuba was imperialism, a pattern of political and military control to serve the interests of U.S. monopolies. It was reinforced by "political capitalism," that is the structure of power and control by a tiny Cuban elite of the life of the country to comport with their own gain and the interests of the U.S. monopolies. The stakes were not just Cuba but all of Latin America:

> As front men for all your monopolies in Latin America, your Department of State is thinking about all of Latin America, and they see quite well that if we Cubans take our own resources and our own talent and labor into our own hands and use them all for our own benefit, as any sovereign people must, then other Latin American countries might get the same fine idea. And do something about it, too.[30]

In response to the "threat" that Cuba represents, the United States has given support to counterrevolutionaries inside and outside Cuba. The counterrevolutionaries inside Cuba are those wealthy citizens who had been the beneficiaries of the old society and hence opposed change. Some opposed Batista because he was a dictator but rejected the radical programs of the revolutionaries, such as the Agrarian Reform Law. Because the vast majority of the Cuban people are the beneficiaries of the new society, there was little support for the counterrevolutionaries. The Cu-

ban revolution was led by young intellectuals, a Cuban"new left,"
and supported by the majority of those living in the countryside.

A more serious threat, the Cuban spokespersons said, came
from U.S. efforts at economic strangulation and military action.
By moving away from a dependency on sugar, the U.S. decision
to stop purchasing Cuban sugar, it was predicted, would fail to
injure the regime. Militarily, an invasion by the U.S. would bring
extensive resistance. Also, because the military threat from the
U.S. was real, Soviet guarantees of Cuba's national security were
important.

From the perspective of the Cubans, the most instructive challenge to the Cuban revolution was a possible replay of the United
States role in the overthrow of the Jacob Arbenz regime in Guatemala. This event, just five years before the defeat of Batista,
illustrated that the United States would do what it could to overthrow regimes that exercised their right to self-determination.
One significant difference between Cuba and the Guatemalan
case, however, was that the Cuban army in place since 1959 was a
revolutionary army, not independent from the regime.It was an
army, not of professional soldiers, but workers and peasants, who
had been participating in revolutionary reconstruction.

The voices of *ListenYankee* argued that Cuban economic and
military ties with the Soviet Union, ironically, were the byproduct
of U.S. imperial policies. First, the Socialist countries had addressed the problem of hunger in their own societies and were
supportive of the efforts of the "hungry bloc" in efforts to solve
their own problems. Second, economic interactions between
Cuba and the Soviet Union were forced upon the former by the
U.S. efforts to isolate Cuba.

Even though Cuban-Soviet relations were good and the Cuban
people were appreciative of the support they received from the
Socialist countries, Cuba had not replaced one form of dependence for another. The Cuban revolution was an authentic, indigenous revolution that was not created by any outsiders. Thus, the
anti-communism reflected in the rhetoric of U.S. policymakers
was misplaced. It was merely a counterrevolutionary tool designed to generate support from U.S. citizens and certain sectors
of the political community in Latin America, much as Secretary
of State John Foster Dulles used the anti-communist rhetoric to
attack the Arbenz regime.

The Cuban commentators end with an injunction to U.S. citizens to call on their leaders to leave "Hands off Cuba!" This requires the realization that Cuba is a sovereign state that has the right to choose the form of government and economy it prefers. To achieve this kind of policy, concerned U.S. citizens have to change the political and economic structure of the United States so that monopolies do not make policy.

In "Note to the Reader, II" C. Wright Mills assessed the arguments made by the composite revolutionary in the prior chapters. In the main, he agreed with the Cubans. Most Latin American countries were governed by an alliance of foreign capital and local elites. In some cases the military were strong centers of power. For the most part, middle classes barely existed and the vast majority of the populations of Latin American countries were poverty stricken. U.S. policy had been to support the status quo in the region for economic reasons. U.S. aid had largely been in the military area. The Cuban revolution then was a new phenomenon in the region.

United States policies toward Cuba are "... based upon a profound ignorance, and are shot through with hysteria." He claimed that these policies "will result in more disgrace and more disaster for the image of my country before Cuba, before Latin America, and before the world."[31] Furthermore these policies were forcing Cuba to align itself with the Socialist bloc.

Mills said that although he was concerned about the reliance of the Cuban revolution on the leadership of one person, he was confident that after the revolution was secure, greater degrees of democracy could emerge in Cuba. The revolution was supported by the peasant majority of the population, in part because basic food requirements were being met. Also, the industrial policies of the new regime were not based upon force used against large sectors of the population. Finally, the young Cuban revolutionaries were energetic, passionate, experimental, and idealistic. All these conditions separated Cuba from other revolutions that had experienced periods of terror and dictatorship. Ultimately *Listen, Yankee* was a plea by C. Wright Mills to the people of the United States to ignore the stridency of Cuban revolutionaries while seriously considering their historically defensible complaints about U.S. imperialism and their just demands for the right to national self-determination.

Cuba in 1960

The three portraits by widely read social analysts and political activists suggest some common elements in the Cuban revolution. First, all the authors document the history of colonialism and neo-colonialism that shaped the Cuban experience. For most Cubans, this history was one of great wealth for a few and immiseration for the many. The root cause of the guerrilla war and its success were attributed to the poverty and powerlessness that Cubans in the 1950s faced, such that the 26th of July Movement was embraced as the hope of the future.

For the authors, the Cuban revolutionaries were stimulated by an animating vision of a new Cuba, one in which national self-determination would be practiced for the first time in four hundred years *and* policies would be based on experiments in social and economic forms to better feed, house, educate, and treat medically the population at large. It was, these writers claimed, a pragmatic revolution not framed by any ideological dogmas. However, because of its stance on the side of the majority, because of its anti-imperialist character, because of the need for strong state action in support of social and economic change, and because of the almost inevitable character of U.S. opposition to the revolution, it would move from a fundamentally national and democratic revolution to a socialist revolution.

The class character of the revolution, the authors argued, was clear. Young intellectuals initiated the military action but the main support came from the peasantry. Huberman and Sweezy, North, and Mills discuss the fact that the peasant character of the revolution is infused with the working class, because many of the rural supporters of the revolution were agricultural workers, not traditional land-owning or land-renting peasants.

While members of other classes joined the revolutionary struggle, they for the most part supported political change but opposed economic change. These participants in the ouster of Batista became the counterrevolutionaries of the 1960s. These counterrevolutionaries were the Cubans still in Havana or later in Miami who would be the tools of United States policy toward Cuba.

For each author, the Cubans were very conscious of the U.S.-sponsored overthrow of the Arbenz government in Guatemala in

1954. They fully expected the United States to use military, covert, and other means to try to destabilize and overthrow the new revolutionary government of Cuba. However, the complexion of historical forces in the world had changed since 1954. Third World peoples looked to the Cuban revolution as an inspiration for their own political actions. The Socialist Bloc by agreeing to trade with and aid Cuba and to defend it militarily, was affording the new revolution a degree of independence and flexibility that it would not have had without the Bloc. The spirit of revolution was spreading throughout Latin America. All this made it less likely that the United States would succeed in its imperial policies.

Lastly, all three authors discussed media distortion of the Cuban revolution. Because of this the citizens of the United States were ill-informed about Cuban history, the real goals of the revolution, and the imperial role the United States had played in Cuba. They did not learn of the critical role U.S. corporations and banks played in the making of U.S. foreign policy.

Several of these themes seem relevant to an examination of the Cuban revolution in the 1990s. First, the underlying dynamic of the revolution was, and still is a spirit of nationalism. Second, U.S. foreign policy toward Cuba is as inalterably opposed to Cuba now as then. Third the media still distorts the Cuban story. (Much coverage of the recently concluded Pan-American Games bears this out. Cuba was framed as a desperately poor country that could only maintain support from the people by engaging in large extravaganzas: the bread and circuses strategy.)

As to elements of the Cuban revolution described by these authors that are different today (and examined in succeeding chapters), the Socialist Bloc as it existed in 1960 no longer exists. Soviet support of the Cuban revolution has been drastically reduced. Consequently, since each author asserted that part of Cuba's freedom, and a reason why Cuba would not become another Guatemala, was a function of the bipolar world, the absence of that world means greater danger to Cuba's future.

Also the authors argued that Cuba represented to the peoples of the Third World an alternative model for their own liberation; an inspiration to movements and regimes. Cuba would rise up from the "hungry bloc" from which it came and others would follow. From the vantage point of the 1990s, progressive regimes and movements are sparse and most Third World regimes have been consigned by virtue of the decline of the Socialist Bloc, worldwide recession, and the international debt to a position of servitude to the international capitalist countries, such that their political options have been dramatically narrowed.

Finally, as Huberman and Sweezy pointed out, the Cuban revolution would retain its large popular support so long as it was able to meet its economic goals. If the economy faltered and people's living conditions worsened, then counterrevolutionaries might gain more support. As will be discussed, the Cuban revolution, by virtue of the dramatic changes in the international system, the socialist world, the Third World, and the international economy, is experiencing economic problems as deep as any experienced since 1959. Whether the revolution can survive in the "new world order" of the 1990s seems more problematic than Cuba's survival in 1960.

Veradero Beach

Chapter 4

The Economics and Politics of the Cuban Revolution: 1959-1986

Introduction

Cuba has been a vast laboratory, always experimenting with new ways of organizing social and economic development to achieve the goals of national self-determination and the people's well-being. This experimentation has not occurred in a vacuum but in the swirl of conflicting domestic and international forces that have to a considerable degree shaped, reshaped, and distorted the policies and goals of the revolution. What this suggests is that economic change and political change are fundamentally interwoven as are domestic and foreign policies. While distinctions are made for ease of description, it must be born in mind that such distinctions belie the interconnectedness of policy and change.

Economic Policies: 1959-1986

Carmelo Mesa-Lago identified five economic problems that afflicted the Cuban economy at the time of the revolution. Economic growth was sluggish, the economy was overwhelmingly dependent upon sugar as its number one money earner, Cuba was singularly dependent on the United States as to trade and investment, Cubans experienced large rates of unemployment and underemployment, and there existed significant inequalities in income, wealth, and basic living conditions, particularly reflected in urban-rural distinctions.[1]

Using these problems as his point of departure, Mesa-Lago described the economic policy currents and debates that characterized Cuba from 1959 to the 1980s. During the first stage, from 1959 through 1960, which he claimed emphasized the elimination of capitalism and the diminution of the market, the young revolutionaries enthusiastically sought to address the multitude of problems with radical shifts in policy.

Major economic programs as exemplified by the Agrarian Reform Law sought to end the gross inequalities in the countryside, increase employment, and diversify the economy by encouraging the production of foodstuffs for domestic consumption. Efforts were made to increase domestic consumption by reducing electricity rates and rent and to free up education and medical services. The state played a much greater role in the economy during this period than before the revolution.

Of course, these radical shifts in policy were occurring in the context of growing resistance to change by wealthy Cubans who turned against the revolution after the May, 1959 agrarian reform program. United States animosities to the new Cuba became visible after May as well. It was during this period, in 1960, that Cuba opened ties to the Soviet Union and established early trade agreements.

Mesa-Lago wrote that the Cuban revolutionaries sought to overcome all five problems in short order. They achieved only mixed results:

> Although a clear policy to promote growth did not exist, moderate growth was achieved by taking advantage of underutilized equipment, stocks, and reserves and by being aided by fair sugar crops and an active government expenditures policy. Little of significance was done to reduce sugar monoculture, and unemployment grew worse in spite of some government measures to stop it. On the other hand, economic dependence on the United States was substantially reduced, and distribution in favor of rural areas and low-income urban groups improved.[2]

Much of the economic policy characterizing this period is reflected in the description of the Cuban revolution referred to in the last chapter. To Sweezy and Huberman, North, and Mills, the Cuban revolutionaries, with buoyant enthusiasm, were creating an active state sector forcing the redistribution of wealth, reinforced by experimental agricultural policies on a variety of fronts.

In retrospect, Mesa-Lago indicated, the enthusiasm of the revolutionaries and the support of the people were not enough to overcome the problems of Cuba's long history, particularly given the worsening of U.S./Cuban relations.

The Cuban economy was pushed quickly toward one dominated by a strong state sector and the seeds were planted for socialism for a number of reasons. First, the Cuban revolutionaries were committed to radical change in the lives of their major constituencies; peasants, workers, and certain sectors of the middle classes. Second, the socio-economic condition of pre-revolutionary Cuba required radical policies if the goals articulated by the revolutionaries were to succeed. Finally, and perhaps most importantly, the United States and its allies among the Cuban bourgeoisie demanded of the new regime policies that would foreclose the possibility of improving the quality of life for peasants and workers and would negate the drive for national self-determination.

As Bray and Harding wrote:

> The foreign dependency, stagnation, monopolization, and unproductivity which characterized the Cuban economy; the enormous technical and capital requirements necessary for the development of any underdeveloped country in the present day; and the absence of a nationalist, autonomous, capitalist class made rapid development of Cuba and a redistribution of wealth to benefit the Cuban masses impossible under capitalism. Only by nationalizing foreign trade, the powerful foreign companies operating in Cuba, and the monopolized private national sector could economic development be effective. In essence, then, development and social equality required socialism.[3]

As a result of the needs of the new Cuban regime and the exigencies forced on the revolutionaries by United States opposition to agrarian reform and nationalizations, the Cubans borrowed much more heavily on ideas and resources from the Socialist Bloc from 1961 to 1963. Edward Boorstein reported that Cubans were encouraged by advisers from Socialist countries to adopt centralized models derived from the Eastern Europe experience. This advice oftentimes was given without sensitivities to the differences between the countries of Eastern Europe and Cuba, and new policies were adapted in mechanistic ways to different local circumstances.[4]

Nevertheless with advice from foreign advisors, collectivization and centralization of the Cuban economy continued. There was a continued drive to industrialize the economy. For a variety of reasons, the production of sugar declined. New enterprises oscillated between improvisation and strong central planning encouraged by the advisors. Planning was made difficult by inadequate information from individual production units and a lack of skilled Cuban economists and statisticians. Thus the major changes projected for the Cuban economy after the initial burst of energy, enthusiasm, and state activism stalled on growing difficulties.

The period between 1964 to 1966 was one of great debate over the fundamental character of the Cuban economy. Particular attention was given to arguments about how Cuban workers should be motivated. For Che Guevara, the Cuban society must commit itself to the creation of "The New Man," the selfless producer for the good of the revolution and the community. For intellectuals close to the Cuban communist party (PSP), in the transition period between capitalism and communism, material incentives would still be needed to motivate workers to produce efficiently and expertly.

The Guevara model assumed that subjective conditions, the raising of the consciousness of workers, could influence objective conditions. Cuba should proceed to eliminate the market and the presumption that wages would be determined by supply and demand. Guevara was urging the full collectivization of the Cuban economy with the state assuming the complete control of economic activity. Guevara envisioned a new economic system in which each would receive according to his or her need and each would produce according to his or her ability. Cuba was going to skip the socialist phase of history, moving directly from capitalism to communism.[5]

Advocates of maintaining material incentives for the short term included Cuban PSP economist Carlos Rafael Rodriquez. He argued that workers could not go beyond the material conditions in which they found themselves. Born and bred under capitalism, Cuban workers could not be weaned away from material motivations by ideological exhortation. Consequently wage and other material incentives were still necessary to secure worker support and energetic participation in the economy of the country. Socialism was a phase in world history which still included the use of the market, profits, interest, differential rents and other elements that were central to capitalism.

Rodriguez called for economic decentralization such that enterprises had more control of decisions involving their own production and were obliged to be profitable. This would ensure that workers and managers would work in ways to maximize efficiency and growth.

During the period of debate, the market socialist approach characterized much of agriculture production and parts of the economy producing for foreign trade while the Guevarist model was applied primarily in industry. Cuba in this period still concentrated on the production of sugar because of comparative advantage in its production and the high demand for it in Europe and the Socialist countries.

In 1966, the Cuban government tilted in the direction of the Guevara model for a variety of reasons including the lack of available resources to emphasize material incentives. The policies adopted during the period from 1966 to 1970 included the full collectivization of the non-state sector with the exception of remaining small private farms. That is, all private businesses and street vendors became part of the state sector. The Cuban state increased its emphasis upon investment in capital accumulation rather than consumer goods. Aside from a small percentage of material rewards offered to model workers for exceptional work, there was a marked shift to moral rather than material incentives. Economic decision-making became more centralized, even though economic decisions were not yet made part of central plans that would govern several years of policy and priorities.

The most significant singular decision made during this period was to commit the society and economy to the production of ten million tons of sugar in 1970. This would have been the largest sugar production in Cuban history. It would allow the Cubans to ship promised but unachieved tonnage to the Soviet Union and would earn enough on the world market to stimulate sizable growth in the industrial sectors of the economy, which had not been a priority since the early 1960s.

All societal resources were put in the service of the ten million ton goal, including shifting labor and machinery, and resources were coupled with exhortations to Cuban workers to produce more for the revolution. To the disappointment of the Castro government, only 8.5 million tons of sugar were actually harvested, in itself the largest amount ever produced in Cuba. The campaign caused major dislocations of resources and labor to achieve the tonnage of sugar that resulted.[7]

The perceived failures of economic policy during this period were coupled with pressure from the Soviet Union to introduce some measure of "market socialism," or responsibility at the enterprise levels to be efficient and profitable, and central planning. Finally, the Cubans still had to contend with the economic and covert challenges from the United States.

The failure of the ten-million ton target in 1970 led Castro to engage in public self-criticism of the policies that surrounded the goal. The policies of the period since 1966, he said, were too idealistic and not grounded in the tangible experiences of other socialist countries. Most critically, changes in the material base of the society must precede changes in the consciousness of the citizenry. In fact, the emphasis on moral incentives and the lack of accountability at the enterprise and work force levels had led to greater absenteeism and declining productivity. It was naive to assume that Cuba could move from capitalism to communism without the transitional stage of socialism.

As a result of the self-criticism, Cuban economic policy shifted in a number of ways. Five-year plans were established by the mid-1970s. State enterprises were decentralized and given more powers to make decisions on productivity. These enterprises were required to generate a profit. Work quotas, wage scales, and incentives were put in place. Modest privatization of the economy re-occurred in the area of small business and services, and private farmers were allowed to sell surpluses to individuals. Sugar was to remain Cuba's major export commodity but emphasis was placed on continued industrialization and the production of other agricultural commodities. Finally, Cuba was admitted into COMECON, the Socialist Bloc common market, in 1972. Thus, the Cuban economy would be incorporated into the socialist division of labor, with Cuba concentrating on the production and export of sugar, nickel, and citrus.

From the mid-1970s to 1986 the Cuban economy experienced modest growth and the material conditions of the lives of Cubans improved. The existence of a "parallel market" where Cubans could buy higher priced goods not available at the rationed stores increased access to consumer goods. Some industrial diversification occurred as well. But despite the stabilization and growth in the Cuban economy, the Cubans saw problems in excessive bureaucratization, corruption, outmoded work standards, an end to voluntary work groups such as the microbrigades, insufficient participation in decision-making by Cuban workers, underrepresentation of women and Afro-Cubans in key economic and political posts, and a decline in revolutionary enthusiasm. These conditions led to the drive for "Rectification" which began in 1986.

Changing Political Conditions in Cuba

The leadership of the Cuban revolution was embodied in the 26th of July Movement that came into being in 1953. It became a broad coalition of political forces representing peasants, workers, students, professionals, and some other elements of the Cuban middle class. While led by former students and professionals, the movement's base of support and military cadres was made up by peasants and agricultural workers. Members of the traditional Cuban communist party, the Partido Socialista Popular or PSP, participated in the struggle to overthrow Batista and indeed had laid the groundwork for the revolution in the struggles of the 1920s, 1930s, and 1940s. While PSP members played an important role in the revolutionary struggle, however, the PSP was not the instrumental organization of the revolution. The 26th of July Movement played that role.

In April 1961, in anticipation of the Bay of Pigs invasion, Fidel Castro declared Cuba a socialist state and in December of that year he announced that he was a Marxist-Leninist. Since the 26th of July Movement had atrophied, the Cuban revolutionaries established in 1961 a new vanguard party that was to incorporate the 26th of July Movement, the Revolutionary Directorate or DR (largely a student organization), and the PSP into the Integrated Revolutionary Organization or ORI. Since the PSP was the only organization of the left with political cadres and structures, it played the major role in building the new party.[8]

ORI militants assumed many positions in government, leaving room for few grassroots members. Consequently, the new party began to lose touch with the population at large and in the process of implementing policy, generated opposition and protest to a variety of policies. Castro in 1962 publicly criticized the authoritarianism and sectarianism of ORI members, thus ending its legitimacy and the first post-revolution effort to institutionalize the revolution.

Castro spoke of a new coalition in July, 1961—the United Party of the Socialist Revolution (PURS) which would become a party uniting the ORI, the PSP, and the DR. After the public criticism of the ORI, PURS became the party expression of the revolution although the authority and charisma of the revolutionary leadership of Fidel Castro dominated the political process, dwarfing any party formation.[9]

In 1965 the organization of PURS was changed and it was renamed the Communist Party of Cuba (PCC). However for the remainder of the decade, the PCC was underdeveloped in terms of membership and presence in factories and communities around the country. The political process remained dominated by the charismatic leadership of Fidel Castro and the revolutionary vanguard inspired by such figures as Che Guevara.

It was not until the 1970s that the revolution was institutionalized and procedures for mass participation in the political life of the country were regularized. The PCC expanded its size and powers, its tasks were defined in conjunction with tasks defined for the state bureaucracy and popular organizations. The Party held its first Congress in 1975, the second in 1980, the third in 1986.[10]

Also Cuba established institutions of "People's Power" in 1976. This consisted of municipal, provincial, and national assemblies selected by popular vote (in the case of the municipal assemblies), and municipal delegate votes to select representatives to the latter two assemblies. Popular participation is encouraged via the mass organizations as well. Preeminent among these are the Committees for the Defense of the Revolution (CDR), the Confederation of Cuban Workers (CTC), The Federation of Cuban Women (FMC), and the National Association of Small Farmers ((ANAP). These and other organizations built memberships in the hundreds of thousands and they operate at local, regional, and national levels. Those that existed in the 1960s served primarily as vehicles to mobilize Cubans to participate in revolutionary projects. Since the 1970s, the mass organizations began to serve also as vehicles for members articulating demands and criticizing ongoing policy and administration.

The sum total of the changes in the political process that occurred after the first decade of the revolution included an institutionalization through a variety of patterns of rule, forms of authority, and political structures and processes by which Cubans could actively participate in the political life of the country. Leo-Grande called the political process of the 1960s "direct democracy."[11] This referred to the symbiotic relationship between leadership and masses that governed this process. Fidel Castro, as the preeminent leader, met with Cubans in the mass or in small groups, and through these meetings policy directives and support emerged.

The changes of the 1970s, writing a new constitution, establishing the legislative process through People's Power, expanding the size, scope, and power of the PCC, and transferring real authority and influence to the mass organizations led to the evolution of Cuban political life from the personal rule of Fidel Castro (although his presence is still of fundamental importance) to institutional rule. These changes in the political realm paralleled the movement toward planning and decentralization in the economic realm. The Cuba of the 1970s and 1980s had changed considerably from the Cuba of the revolution proper and the shifting currents of policy and behavior in the 1960s.

Cuban Foreign Policy From 1959 to the 1980s

The goals of the new revolutionary regime that came to power in 1959, as reflected in the ideology and perspectives of the revolutionary leadership and the coalition of peasants, workers, students, and others, included the effort to achieve national self-determination and the betterment of the living conditions for the vast majority of Cubans. The achievement of these goals inevitably meant confrontation with the United States because of the traditional U.S. control of Cuba's economic and political life and the conflict between U.S. corporate profits and the need to create higher wages, full employment, and much expanded state services for the Cuban citizenry, which would require taxation of investors and land owners.

U.S. hostility was reflected in the suspiciousness the Eisenhower administration showed the Cuban revolutionaries as they mobilized in the mountains to defeat the Batista armies. The hostility became more visible after Fidel Castro's visit to the United States in April, 1959. While Castro did not formally request economic assistance, the Administration made it clear that such aid would not be forthcoming and if Cuba wished outside aid it could apply for loans from the International Monetary Fund. Castro had called for a Marshall Plan for Latin America but this proposal was dismissed by the U.S. administration.[12]

When Castro returned home after his U.S. visit, he instituted the controversial Agrarian Reform Law which limited the amount of land any individual or corporation could own to 1,000 acres, a move that attacked the huge land holdings of Cuban and foreign investors. It is at this point that the more conservative elements of the revolutionary coalition withdrew and many began to participate in covert operations to undermine and overthrow the Cuban government. By the fall, 1959, the United States was giving encouragement and support to such efforts.

The pattern of escalating conflict with the United States then proceeded with great speed. Expecting that the United States would seek to strangle the new reformist regime economically, the Cuban government established formal diplomatic relations and trade agreements with the Soviet Union in the spring, 1960. When U.S. oil companies refused to refine oil received from the Soviet Union, the Cuban government seized the refineries. The U.S. responded with the dramatic cut in the quota of sugar purchased from Cuba. Cuba then nationalized public utilities and other companies owned by the U.S. and the U.S. instituted an economic embargo and blockade of Cuba that continues to the present. Formal diplomatic relations were ended in January 1961.[13]

By 1961, the United States was fully involved in programs to destabilize Cuba and to overthrow the new revolutionary regime. The first approach was to encourage and support *internal* forces committed to the end of the revolution. When the internal strategy failed, the U.S. turned more fully to an *external* strategy. The paradigmatic external strategy was the financing and training of a military force to invade Cuba, defeat the Cuban army, and seize state power. The program was begun in March, 1960 as a result of a directive from President Eisenhower and culminated in the failed Bay of Pigs invasion in April of 1961, under John F. Kennedy's administration.[14]

Consequently, a first concern of Cuban policymakers, and the single most critical shaping experience of the revolution, was the hostility of the United States. Cuba had to establish economic and political relations with other countries to counter the economic blockade that was being imposed by the United States (This blockade involved extensive efforts by the United States to get its allies to end all relations with Cuba. This achieved only partial success in the 1960s and 1970s).[15] Given the bipolar structure of international relations, Cuba logically moved toward closer ties with the Soviet Union.

Since 1960 the Soviet Union provided significant amounts of economic and military assistance to Cuba and purchased much of the sugar crop that historically had been purchased by the United States. The Soviet Union indicated it would militarily defend Cuba from assault by the United States. The Cuban missile crisis of 1962 resulted from U.S. opposition to the Soviet military assistance to Cuba and a nuclear military presence on Cuban soil.[16]

Relations with the Soviet Union, however, were not always smooth during the thirty-one years of the revolution. In the 1960s, Cuba vigorously supported revolutionary movements in Latin America and Africa, a stance that the more conservative Soviet Union sometimes opposed.[17] Further, the periodic experiments with Guevara's ideas in the economy made Soviet economists uncomfortable. Also there were occasions when Soviet action in reference to Cuba was taken without the support or knowledge of Cuban decision makers; for example the Soviets negotiated a solution to the missile crisis without consulting the Cubans.

On some occasions, Cuban foreign policy influenced the Soviets to act rather than the Soviets directing Cuba's policies. Cuba's desire to defend the MPLA government in Angola led the former to send arms and aid when Angola was attacked by Angolan contras led by Jonas Savimbi.[18] Soviet support was to follow.

Despite the material support the Soviet Union has given to the revolution, Cuban/Soviet relations were based on a considerable degree of Cuban independence. Only under extreme pressure has Cuba agreed to policies that it would ordinarily not support, such as the Soviet military invasion of Czechoslovakia in 1968.

Perhaps the most significant constraint on Cuba derivable from its relations with the Socialist Bloc had to do with Cuba's consignment to sugar production as part of the socialist division of labor in COMECON. Distortions based on a one-crop economy persisted because of Cuba's role in the Eastern European common market.

The direction of Cuban foreign policy was shaped by expediency and principle. The tilt toward the Soviet Union, while to some degree caused by ideological affinities, resulted largely from pragmatic considerations involving military and economic survival. Pragmatic *and* principled or ideological motivations shaped Cuba's response to the Third World as well.[19] Cuba, in the 1960s, supported guerrilla movements in Latin America in those countries that joined the U.S. effort to crush the revolution. The Organization of American States expelled Cuba over the objections of some countries such as Mexico. Cuba supported guerrilla movements in several of the OAS states but abstained from giving support to anti-government activists in Mexico.

In the 1970s, Cuba gave significant support to revolutionary governments in Africa and made major military commitments to Angola and Ethiopia. In the Africa case (and to the Latin American case as well), Cuban policy was motivated by principles of international solidarity and historic and cultural links. Cuba's unusually large presence in Africa and Latin America, for a country its size and wealth, entailed the sending of doctors, teachers, construction workers, and other technical advisers as well as troops and military hardware. Furthermore, Third World youth were invited to pursue educational programs in Cuba as well.

The result of Cuba's visible presence in the international arena, particularly in the Third World, led it to be a leader of the Non-Aligned Movement. The sixth non-aligned summit meeting was held in Havana in the fall of 1979. Later, Cuba would try to mobilize debt-poor Third World countries to launch an economic counteroffensive against the industrial capitalist world. For Cuba, there was a natural affinity toward the countries of Asia, Africa, and Latin America because they all shared common colonial and neo-colonial experiences and were desperately seeking social and economic development.

By the 1970s, with the relative success of Cuba's efforts to survive the assault from the United States, Cuba decreased its level of support for Third World revolutionary movements, especially in Latin America. Pressures from the Soviet Union also had an effect upon Cuba's international activities. As a result relations between Cuba and Latin America improved in the 1970s and 1980s. In 1982, when the United States supported Great Britain's military effort to reestablish control of the Falkland Islands from Argentinean challenge, Cuba joined all other Latin American states in opposing British and U.S. policies. The Pinochet dictatorship and the Cuban socialist regime shared common positions against U.S. imperial policies directed against another Latin American nation.

Therefore, Cuban foreign policy was governed to a considerable degree by its need to protect itself from United States economic, political, and military hostility. It was this hostility that fostered the evolving close relationship between Cuba and the Soviet Union leading ultimately to Cuba's incorporation into the Socialist Bloc. It is important to note however that the Cuba/Soviet relationship was furthered by shared principles and ideology.

Cuba's principled solidarity with Third World peoples was reflected in its support of revolutionary movements in the 1960s and revolutionary regimes in the 1970s and 1980s. Also, Cuban policy was designed to support a bloc of Third World nations that, it was hoped, could be weaned away from dependent ties on the industrial capitalist countries of the "north." Cuban policy was based on the assumption that the tiny island shared a common history, place in the international economy, and destiny as other countries in the Third World. If they could act in common, the hegemony of western imperial powers, particularly the United States, could be effectively challenged.

While standing firm in its commitment to national self-determination and the goal of creating its own economic path, Cuban foreign policy did change over the years as historical circumstance dictated. First, with the willingness of Latin American countries to resume economic and political relations in the 1970s and 1980s, Cuba ended its support for guerrilla movements and developed agreements often with conservative and authoritarian regimes. Second, Cuba, by the 1970s, developed foreign policies deemed less objectionable to the Soviet Union. The latter had for several years sought to discourage Cubans from allying themselves with guerrilla movements.

Finally, Cuba expressed a willingness to engage in serious ne-
gotiation with the United States with an eye toward tension reduction. The period from 1974 to 1979 was one of reduced animosities as reflected in the establishment of Cuban and United
States "interest sections" in the two countries' respective capitals.
President Carter also allowed U.S. citizens to tour in Cuba for the
first time in fifteen years. However, because of Cuba's support of
the Angolan and Ethiopian regimes and its leadership role in the
non-aligned movement, Carter and then Reagan rekindled the
Cold War toward Cuba, and Cuba, for reasons of principle, refused to withdraw from its participation in African and Third
World affairs.

Conclusion

Taken together, Cuban domestic and foreign policies and its
political process have changed since 1959 as a result of the dialec-
tical interconnection between them, the needs of the Cuban people, and the resistance of the United States. To some degree the
revolutionary zeal of the first decade characterized by great debates in economic policy, a spontaneous and mass-based politics,
and support for revolutionaries around the world, changed in the
1970s and 1980s. By the 1970s economic planning, central direction and enterprise flexibility, and incentive policies had become
institutionalized. Similarly, political participation had become
regularized through the Cuban Communist Party, popular assemblies, and mass organizations. Foreign policies were shaped by
both pragmatic considerations, such as the willingness of other
countries to recognize and trade with Cuba, and ideology, international solidarity with Third World peoples.

What remained the same throughout the period from 1959 to
the 1980s was a commitment to the fundamental goals of national self-determination and economic betterment. To achieve
these goals, the Cubans remained flexible in their response to
economic needs and foreign policy challenges.

Chapter 5

Cuba and the Changing International System: 1986-1991

Introduction

President Reagan's first term reflected a foreign policy toward socialist countries and progressive Third World nations and movements that was as hostile and as militaristic as any post-World War II administration. The prospects for nuclear and conventional war were high and conversely the chances of any arms control negotiations and diminution of regional wars seemed negligible. In defense against this militancy renewed by the United States, after the fall of the Shah of Iran in 1979 but heightened after Reagan assumed the presidency in 1981, the Soviet Union maintained its own arms strength and supported allies in South and Southeast Asia, Southern Africa, the Middle East, and Central America and the Caribbean.[1]

Soviet economic and military relations with Cuba remained strong. Cuba for its part sought to convince fellow members of the non-aligned countries movement that their interests would be best served by collaboration with the Soviet Union. While many non-aligned nations resisted this position, Soviet influence throughout the international system remained strong.

The international atmosphere began to change after 1985. A new regime came to power in the Soviet Union, led by Mikhail Gorbachev. Burdened with high defense expenditures, an overly centralized and bureaucratized economic system, and declining levels of development, Gorbachev began a process of creative diplomacy designed to reduce Cold War tensions so that the defense drain on Soviet society and the Socialist Bloc could be reduced. Consequently the Soviet Union established a posture that emphasized the need for the reversal of the arms race and the reduction of conflicts in Asia, the Middle East, Southern Africa, and Central America. By 1988, the changes in Soviet foreign *and* domestic policy had set in motion a dynamic for change all across Eastern Europe, and later the Soviet Union itself, that culminated in the dissolution of the Socialist Bloc. Because of the radical changes, the traditional division of Europe seemed anachronistic.

While hardliners among Reagan and Bush advisors worked to undermine the deescalation of tensions between East and West, the United States was forced by Gorbachev's popularity in Western Europe and the radical changes in Eastern Europe to respond in kind. Some measure of tension reduction was achieved by 1988 with arms negotiations and agreements to defuse so-called "regional trouble spots." However, with the further disintegration of the Socialist Bloc and the Soviet Union itself, the United States sought to overcome its own economic problems by reasserting its military hegemony in a world of declining bipolarity. The invasion of Panama in December, 1989 was a trial balloon for the larger and more brutal war against Iraq in January, 1991, a war that was legitimized by the creation of a United Nations coalition including the Soviet Union.

Significantly, Cuba was one of only two states in the UN Security Council to stand against the U.S. military policy against Iraq. The new international system, which included an end to socialism in Europe and a revived U.S. militarism, presented Cuba with the most serious challenges to its existence since 1959. It remained to be seen whether Cuba could survive in a world of capitalist powers and capitalist dependencies, and constantly threatened by a U.S. military superpower unleashed twice in two years against weak Third World countries.

The Soviet Peace Offensive

There was little indication when the second Reagan term began that United States/Soviet relations would begin to improve at a surprising pace. In January 1985, Secretary of State George Schultz and Foreign Minister Gromyko had initiated talks that led to the resumption of arms negotiations on the reduction of intercontinental and intermediate range missiles but no one expected that these negotiations, officially started in Geneva in March, would bear fruit. The Reagan offensive program against the socialist states and progressive Third World peoples in the 1980s and the traditional defensive Soviet response did not suggest that change was likely.

Gorbachev unleashed a movement of large-scale social change within the Soviet Union that reverberated in unpredictable ways throughout the then socialist world. Significantly, Soviet foreign policy began to force the United States to modify its own armaments policies.

The Gorbachev diplomatic offensive began within a month of his assumption of office in 1985 and continued into the Bush Administration. Washington was consistently seen as the great power that was fearful that peace might break out. Some of the Gorbachev proposals to deescalate the arms race and East/West tensions had been made by prior Soviet regimes, but the steady pace of those made after 1985 and the way in which they were presented left the impression with Europeans, many U.S. citizens and others that the openness was an entirely new phenomena.

A central element of Gorbachev's "new thinking" was the idea that certain human values, such as survival, took precedence over class struggle. The Soviet leader argued that the existence of nuclear weapons made war prevention the primary priority of humankind and that therefore achieving a reduction in tensions and armaments between the great powers constituted the fundamental goal of Soviet foreign policy. Since conventional war between the two powers would most probably escalate to nuclear war, the practical necessity of the epoch required agreements to end the prospect of war between them. While competition between peoples, cultures, ideologies, and economic systems would remain, it of necessity needed to be peaceful.[2]

Applying the idea of the universal value of human survival embodied in "the new thinking" was the idea of "reasonable sufficiency" as to national security.[3] This concept implied that Soviet defense capabilities would be based on the capacity to respond adequately to attacks by aggressors but it challenged the need for superiority or even parity with the United States to defend itself. Defense needs, it was felt, should be designed to minimize the negative impact on the domestic economy and should not be of a magnitude to threaten other countries. "Reasonable sufficiency" ideas led the Soviet Union to make dramatic proposals for reducing armaments and sometimes to take unilateral actions to spur on the process.

The Gorbachev "new thinking" stimulated changing relations with and concerns about Europe, China, and Third World countries. Gorbachev drew European states into the tension reduction process independent of the United States, a policy that generated much enthusiasm among peace-minded West European peoples. He expanded relations with the Peoples Republic of China to reduce the intense hostilities that had existed between the two countries for decades.

Finally, and most critical for Cuba, Gorbachev began the process of reducing Soviet presence in the Third World. Some Gorbachev advisors even argued that the Soviet support for progressive governments in the Third World stimulated conflict with the U.S. in these areas.[4] Essentially, proponents of this thesis were stating that major Third World conflicts such as in Vietnam or Angola had occurred because the Soviet Union had a presence there rather than because of U.S. aggression. As the years passed, Soviet policy seemed to be increasingly based on a repudiation of its past. These shifts in policy, while defusing some of the most dangerous Cold War tensions, would be increasingly seen from Cuba as an ominous development in terms of its own security.

The United States Responds to the Soviet Peace Offensive

The Carter Administration tilted toward Cold War II in 1979 after the fall of the Shah of Iran. Iran had been a critical "gendarme state" in the vital Persian Gulf area whose role was to represent U.S. geopolitical and economic interests. His precipitous fall and subsequent revolutions in Grenada and Nicaragua and revolutionary ferment in El Salvador convinced Carter policymakers that the decline of U.S. hegemony had to be reversed. The taking of U.S. hostages in Teheran in November, 1979 and the Soviet troop commitment to save a faltering ally in Afghanistan in December, led President Carter to declare in January 1980 that the Cold War would be resumed.[5]

During the 1980 presidential campaign and during the first years in office, President Reagan expanded the U.S. military and ideological struggle against the Soviet Union and progressive regimes around the world. It was proclaimed that the U.S. policy was to defeat international terrorism and that the number one purveyor of terrorism around the world was the Soviet Union either directly or through its "surrogates." Perhaps the number one "surrogate" was Cuba. Reagan also proclaimed that the Soviet Union represented an "evil empire" and that communism was a passing phase in human history.[6]

To support his ideological pronouncements, President Reagan introduced the largest peacetime escalation of defense spending in United States history. Later he committed the U.S. to the construction of a space defense shield known as the Strategic Defense Initiative or SDI. This forced the Soviet Union into an extension of the arms race that ultimately was fatal to its economy.

Along with the struggle against the Soviet Union, President Reagan declared a commitment to fight against progressive movements all around the world and to avoid another embarrassment such as Vietnam, the struggle would be carried out through "Low Intensity Conflict." The United States directly and indirectly participated in violent conflicts in Asia, Africa, the Middle East, and Latin America.

In the Western Hemisphere, the Reagan Administration targeted Nicaragua for destabilization by supporting a brutal contra army. Reagan supported an equally brutal military as the governments of El Salvador sought to crush a rebel movement. In defense of its policies, the United States claimed that the Nicaragua government and the Salvador rebels, the Farabundo Marti Liberation Front or FMLN, were the creation of Cuba. On occasion, Reagan spokespersons threatened to "go to the source," which meant military action against Cuba.[7]

With this background, the U.S. reaction to the Soviet peace offensive between 1985 and 1989 was contradictory, suggesting a reluctance of the former to give up the stereotypes of the Soviet Union that served to justify high defense expenditures and an interventionist foreign policy. For example, shortly after Secretary of State Schultz and Foreign Minister Gromyko agreed to resume arms talks in January, 1985, President Reagan renewed charges that the Soviet Union was violating prior arms agreements. He also defended the necessity of the United States to continue development of the Strategic Defense Initiative.

Over the course of the next three years the Soviets would unilaterally act to promote the peace process; for example, to declare a moratorium on nuclear testing and to halt the deployment of new intermediate range missiles in Eastern Europe. The United States often criticized these actions and the myriad of arms control proposals coming from Moscow, but President Reagan did reluctantly participate in summit negotiations with President Gorbachev in 1985, 1986, 1987, and 1988. Some modest agreements were reached on cultural exchanges. Meanwhile Gorbachev was expanding his network of communications with Western business persons to encourage foreign investment.

Finally, in early December, 1987, Gorbachev visited the United States and the two leaders signed the Intermediate Nuclear Force Treaty (INF). It required the dismantling of 2,611 Soviet and U.S. intermediate and short range missiles in Europe and included verification visits for 13 years. Also the two leaders discussed issues dividing the nations, including the presence of Soviet troops in Afghanistan. In the era of the "evil empire," the Reagan Administration had finally committed itself to a modest, but symbolically important, agreement to reduce arms from the arsenals of the two powers. Despite the resistance of the United States, the INF treaty set in motion an arms reduction dynamic in international diplomacy that was to continue into the Bush Administration.

The Soviets and their allies provided most of the initiatives to reduce tensions around the world in 1988. For example, the Soviet Union removed 30 SS-12 missiles from the then German Democratic Republic, Vietnam announced a projected complete withdrawal of its troops from Cambodia by 1990, and Afghanistan and the Soviet Union signed an agreement with Pakistan and the United States to withdraw Soviet troops from Afghanistan by February, 1989, while the countries supporting the Afghan rebels were to end their military aid to them.

Significant moves were taken in December, 1988 with the Gorbachev announcement at the United Nations that the Soviet Union was reducing its conventional force capability by 500,000 troops, or 20 percent of its force level. Along with the troop reduction the Soviets would reduce their material forces by 10,000 tanks, 8,500 artillery pieces, and 800 combat aircraft.

Shortly after the UN trip (which included a visit with President Reagan), Cuba, Angola, and South Africa completed a treaty promising a phased withdrawal of Cuban troops from Angola, a reduction of South African troops in Namibia, and elections for a parliament in Namibia leading to the writing of a constitution and Namibian independence. Unfortunately, the Angolan contra force known as UNITA was not incorporated in the treaty and consequently the civil war in Angola continued.

The Bush Administration seemed as reluctant to respond to Soviet diplomatic initiatives in 1989 as had been the Reagan Administration since 1985, but over the next two years changes in Eastern Europe, the demise of socialist states, and the disintegration of the Soviet Union led U.S. policymakers to the view that indeed the Cold War was over and that the "Soviet Bloc" and the "evil empire" no longer existed. With the Soviets internal problems and withdrawal from its presence in parts of the Third World, the deterrence against U.S. militarism had dissipated.

The United States, for its part, was experiencing the latest phase of a long economic decline in the international capitalist system born of competition from others states, indebtedness, technological inferiority as compared to Europe and Japan, a declining industrial base and economic infrastructure, and a systemic shift from investments in production to speculative transactions.[8] Among the industrial capitalist powers, the United States preeminence was registered more in its military superiority rather than its economic capability. The end to the Cold War was leading to demands for a reduction in the $300 billion arms budget, which had stimulated the economic recovery of the 1980s.

With a stagnating economy confronting European and Japanese competition and the threatened reduction in the arms industry, U.S. policymakers pursued a foreign policy of trying to reestablish U.S. global hegemony by virtue of its military superiority. In December, 1989, President Bush sent troops into Panama to defeat the armies of General Manuel Noriega and to kidnap him to go on trial in Miami for drug smuggling. The U.S. invasion occurred some three years after the United States began a public crusade to portray Noriega as a demon in the post-evil empire era. Noriega, the former CIA payroller, was reframed in the media as the major cause of the U.S. drug problem.

The next demon, also a former U.S. payroller, was Saddam Hussein, leader of Iraq. Shortly after Iraq invaded Kuwait in August, 1990, the United States defined Iraq as a threat to the whole region. After control of Kuwait was consolidated, Iraq would invade Saudi Arabia, it was argued. No evidence to support this was presented.

While Iraq and various international actors proposed negotiations to end the crisis from late August to January, 1991, the United States refused to take them seriously and proceeded to build a U.N. coalition to authorize the use of force against Iraq. The coalition consisted of the U.S. European allies and Third World countries such as Egypt who were seriously compromised by international debt. Also rich oil sheiks from Kuwait and Saudi Arabia encouraged the U.S. military approach because of their fear of Sadam Hussein's popularity with Arab peoples around the region.

Only two nations consistently opposed the U.S. led coalition in the United Nations, Yemen and Cuba. With the crumbling Soviet Union as a coalition partner, it was clear that Cuba was increasingly being alienated from its traditional socialist ally and was isolated from its natural constituency among Third World countries. Cuba was taking a position that Third World countries historically would have taken if they had not become so completely dependent upon the industrial capitalist states through indebtedness and the dream of securing foreign investors in their countries. Cuba, on the other hand, acted on principle by opposing militarism even though it may have cost itself a better relationship with the United States.

Finally on January 15, 1991, the war started, as the most militarily powerful nation in world history began a massive bombardment of Iraq. Within six weeks the war was over and two hundred thousand Iraqis had been killed and untold thousands more would die of starvation and disease in the months ahead because of the complete destruction of the Iraqi economic and public infrastructure by U.S. and allied air power. Moreover, the military victory, despite the devastation, ecological spoilation, and social disintegration in the region, reinforced the U.S. commitment to establish its military hegemony in the international system. Bush captured this sentiment when he said at a press conference that Sadam Hussein and other dictators must learn "that what we say goes."[9] That in substance was the Bush "new world order."

United States Policy Toward Cuba in the 1980s

The Reagan Administration threatened to "go to the source" of the instabilities in Central America; that is, Cuba. It also carried out policies short of war to destroy the Cuban revolution. It canceled the right of U.S. citizens, other than selected categories of people, Cuban-Americans, researchers, and journalists, to visit Cuba. No longer could U.S. citizens tour in Cuba, leaving dollars that would help its economy. In 1983, the Reagan Administration sent marines to Grenada to end revolutionary politics there and fought Cuban construction workers who had been working there to complete a new airport. In 1985, the Reagan Administration established "Radio Marti," to beam anti-revolutionary propaganda to the Cuban people.

President Bush continued the harassment of Cuba. In January, 1989, a U.S. Coast Guard ship fired on a Cuban vessel in the Gulf of Mexico demanding to board it to search for drugs. The Cuban officers resisted the attack and upon entering Mexican waters allowed the ship to be searched for drugs. Of course none could be found. Bush then introduced "TV Martí," an effort to transmit anti-Cuban broadcasts to Cuban television watchers in violation of international telecommunication rules about national sovereignty. Despite Cuba's jamming of these broadcasts, Congress continued to fund the television station.

Maneuvers have also been carried out in the Caribbean including overflights of the island and simulated evacuations of the U.S. base at Guantanamo. The idea is to keep the threat of a U.S. invasion alive so that Cuba will continue to spend scarce resources on military equipment and personnel. Further, Congresspersons closely allied with the rightwing Cuban lobby continued to introduce legislative proposals to further tighten the economic embargo against Cuba.

Finally, Bush policymakers, including the president's sons, have worked closely with the U.S. government funded rightwing Cuban American National Foundation, which has already made plans to return property to former property owners once the revolution collapses. This group, influential in policymaking, represents those Cubans who wish to take the country back to the Batista era.

Therefore United States policy toward Cuba remained the same in the 1980s and 1990s as it had been since 1959: military threat, economic blockade, efforts at international ostracism, and, where possible, covert operations. This was true despite the radical changes in the international system, changes in Cuban foreign policy, and changes in what could have been seen years ago as a threat to national security. The ultimate threat that has existed since 1959 remains however; the threat of a good example. Cuba, for all its flaws, has represented a model for national self-determination, equality, and human need fulfillment for Third World countries that is not based on a dependent capitalist model of economic growth.

Cuban Rectification: Responses to Economic and Political Stagnation

Cuba can be conceptualized as a social laboratory, one in which experimentation and change is as characteristic as tradition and stability. The experimental method meant that as mistakes were identified policymakers would develop new programs to rectify or eliminate the errors.

The political and economic system that was put in place in Cuba in the 1970s was increasingly seen in the 1980s as fraught with problems. Fidel Castro noted this fact at the initial session of the Third Party Congress of the Cuban Communist Party. He spoke at length of the economic, political, and ideological mistakes that had become manifest since the last major policy changes that occurred in the 1970s. He called for a vast "Rectification Campaign" to overcome the flaws in the economic and political order. The criticisms and some proposed changes then were committed to print, the Congress suspended, and debate throughout the society encouraged. The Congress reconvened in late November, 1986 to develop and operationalize policies for the years ahead.[10]

Economically, the System of Economic Management and Planning (SDPE), in place from 1976 to 1986, had generated corruption, bureaucracy, erroneous reporting of production figures, inordinately low work production norms, the production of poor quality goods and other problems. Perhaps most importantly, the spirit of the revolution was being lost in materialism and individualism. Also, the Cuban leadership condemned (and canceled) the market in agricultural goods that, it was claimed, had created a class of wealthy distributors of foodstuffs. To Castro and others the farmers' market was planting the seeds for capitalism and social inequality's return.

Politically, the institutions of popular power and the mass organizations had become too centralized and bureaucratic so that input from the masses of Cuban citizens was being stifled.

The Cuban Communist Party dominated the state institutions and the municipal, provincial, and national assemblies. Leaders were often too old and out of touch with grassroots sentiments. Women, Afro-Cubans, and young people were underrepresented in the political process.

Ideologically, Cuban zeal in support of the revolution had dwindled as a result of excessive materialism in Cuban life, images of consumerism from the United States, complaints about shortages of goods, and the general improvements in the quality of life that had led some Cubans to forget the enormous gains since the revolution. Economic difficulties, an overemphasis on material incentives, and propaganda campaigns from the United States, reduced the level of revolutionary consciousness that could only be repaired with renewed education. As Castro suggested:

> I have seen the example of what was happening to us: the blind belief—or it began to be blind—that the construction of socialism is basically a question of mechanisms. As I pointed out (at a recent meeting with Cuban journalists).... I think that the construction of socialism and communism is essentially a political task and a revolutionary task. It must be fundamentally the fruit of the development of an awareness and educating people for socialism and communism.[11]

In response then at the levels of economics, politics, and ideology, a rectification campaign was put in place in late 1986 designed to achieve in Castro's words, a "consciousness, a communist spirit" to overcome economic stagnation, bureaucratization, corruption, low worker productivity, and the existence of a sense of demoralization among sectors of the population. The image of Che Guevara, the selfless fighter for freedom and human dignity, was again presented as the exemplar of the communist spirit that

Cubans should aspire too. While speaking against the idealist errors of the 1960s, the rectification campaign sought a return in significant ways to the era of moral incentives of which Guevara was the leading advocate.

The campaign after 1986 occurred on a variety of fronts. As to economic changes, microbrigades were reinstituted and projects involving the construction of housing, day care facilities, and other public buildings led to large numbers of new facilities. Greater worker input in factories and agricultural enterprises was encouraged. Work norms were adjusted. The spirit of volunteer-ism in production was encouraged. Finally, bureaucratic ineffi-ciencies and governmental waste were attacked.[12]

As to politics, some members of the highest organs of the CCP were dismissed for poor performance. Representation of women, Blacks, and young people were increased. Efforts to improve grassroots meetings and input into the political process were en-couraged. Also the media was encouraged to be more critical of ongoing institutions. Both in response to the CCP Congress documents of 1986 and the call for the Fourth Party Congress in 1991, assemblies of workers and others were encouraged to meet and discuss the issues facing Cuba. Cuban authorities claimed that positions adopted by some 80,000 assemblies in anticipation of the Fourth Party Congress of the CCP were tabulated and would influence decisions made. The process of "bottom-up" po-litical influence was encouraged in the mass organizations as well to overcome their propensity to be hierarchical, and conduits for party policies rather than interest groups representing grassroots constituencies.

As to ideology, the regime sought through exhortation, sym-bolism, and invitations to participation to rekindle the revolution-ary spirit of Che Guevara. Efforts were made to underscore revo-lutionary Cuba's refusal to transform itself into capitalism as it seemed to be occurring in the Eastern European states and the Soviet Union. The closure of the farmers' markets, as much as appeals to the spirit of Che, illustrated the fact that the rectifica-tion campaign was not like perestroika and glasnost. To the Cu-ban regime, the social changes needed in the 1980s and beyond were designed to move closer to communism, not away from it. However, underlying the defiant commitment to Cuba's socialist revolution was an equally defiant commitment by Cubans to defend their homeland and their right to national self-determination. Thus the ideological thrust of the rectification campaign comported with the 400-year drive of Cubans to achieve and maintain their independence. It is this commonality that made Cuba's Marxist-Leninist ideology truly indigenous.

Cuba and the Changing International System

In 1989, the once united and economically viable Socialist Bloc began to crumble. At first, stimulated by the Gorbachev reforms in the Soviet Union, democratic socialists in each Eastern European country were overwhelmed by anti-communist currents and popular criticism of economic stagnation and political authoritarianism at home. Consequently, one by one the regimes of Eastern Europe fell and local communist parties were replaced. By 1991, the Soviet Union itself was fraught with turmoil and disintegration, further fueled by a failed attempted coup against Michael Gorbachev in August, 1991. As a result of popular resistance and the return of Gorbachev, the Soviet Communist Party itself was forced out of a leadership position in the political system.

The disintegration of Eastern Europe and the Soviet Union in such a short period of time was a wrenching experience for the Cubans. Eighty-three per cent of Cuba's trade before 1989 was with the Socialist Bloc, 70 per cent of which was with the Soviet Union. As a result of Cuba's place in the socialist division of labor, it had been committed primarily to the production of a few commodities for export, particularly sugar and nickel. Cuba imported machinery, transportation vehicles, wheat, rice, and most critically oil. Further, because of energy efficiencies in the 1980s, Cuba had been able to resell some oil imported from the Soviet Union on the world market to earn scarce foreign exchange.

Consequently, the Cuban regime was forced to initiate a "special period" in 1989 to adapt to the declining trade, the increasing failure of the Soviet system to deliver contracted goods, reductions in Soviet assistance, scarcities in basic commodities acquired from abroad such as oil, and the need to reorient itself away from the socialist division of labor. The special period that began in 1989 required these radical changes in economic policy and priorities at the same time that the United States cold war against Cuba was heating up and Cuba was being isolated in the international system because of its principled stand in opposition to the United Nations Gulf War policy. Basically Cuba had to learn to cope with a collapsed Socialist Bloc, dramatically weakened and compromised Third World solidarity, and growing U.S. hostilities.

The Cuban response, which may or may not guarantee Cuba's survival, was multifaceted. First, Cuba continued its foreign policy of many years to cultivate alternative political and economic relations around the world. Diplomatically, Cuba had established diplomatic relations with more countries than ever before. Most Latin American members of the Organization of American States had reestablished relations with Cuba and preferred that Cuba be readmitted into the OAS. Cuba had established trade agreements with a variety of nations in Latin America and elsewhere. This was facilitated by a broadening of Cuba's export platform to include biotechnology, pharmaceuticals, and other commodities along with sugar and nickel.

Of potential significance to Cuba's future, it signed trade agreements with China worth $800 million and China had provided Cuba with 200,000 bicycles for mass distribution. Consequently, Cuba speeded up its longer term effort to diversify its political and economic ties.

Also, in short order, Cuba began an economic restructuring that had as its goal reducing its external dependency. The Cuban government marshalled resources for a dramatic increase in the production of foodstuffs for domestic consumption. Residents of the Havana province were especially urged to become self-sufficient in food production. Brigades of volunteers were enlisted for short or long periods to grow and harvest crops on the outskirts of Havana.

Further, the Cubans continued research and development leading to an expanded biotechnology industry for export. Cubans produced machines for large-scale blood tests and vaccines to prevent Meningitis B for sale on the world market. They also produced pharmaceuticals for sale. The biotechnology export industry was approaching tobacco in its foreign earnings capacity.

Cognizant of its complex impacts on Cuban life, the government committed itself to expanding a tourist industry. With joint venture investments from Spain, Germany, and Great Britain the

Cubans increased tourist travel to its lovely beaches and country-side and hoped to increase the number of tourists by a factor of five by the onset of the next century. Tourism then would challenge sugar as the primary earner of foreign currency.

Along with efforts to diversify the Cuban economy, energy conservation measures were taken that seriously compromised production and the comforts of the Cuban people. As noted, Cuba imported 200,000 bicycles from China, which were distributed across the population and to groups, like university students, who traditionally used public transportation. This would partially substitute for decaying buses and the reduction in public transportation.

Other fuel economy measures included using pack animals to replace tractors to save fuel. Factories were put on shorter work weeks to reduce energy consumption and many construction projects were halted because of the special period. Cuts were made in the importation of energy inefficient products such as refrigerators and air conditioners. Consequently, Cuba during the special period was attempting to diversify its trade partners and exports, substituting domestic food production for imports, and extending planning to maximize energy efficiency. Finally, virtually all commodities in the country were rationed to insure that the scarce resources would be shared equitably.

Discussions of the adequacies and inadequacies of the policies of the special period and the continued rectification campaign were to be discussed at the Fourth Party Congress of the Cuban Communist Party in October, 1991. The Congress was to be held a month after President Gorbachev announced to the world that the Soviet Union would be withdrawing its military support and Soviet soldiers from Cuba. He also hinted at the possibility that the Soviet Union would be ending its close economic relationship with Cuba as well. These announcements were greeted with glee among the most reactionary elements of the Cuban American community and the Bush administration. The U.S. government and the Cuban American National Foundation had been pressuring the Soviets to end their ties with Cuba every since the onset of Gorbachev's "new thinking."

How the Cuban people were bearing up under the strain brought on by the radical changes in the international system would be seen as the PCC deliberated the future of the revolution at the Fourth Congress. There is no question that this period was one of the greatest challenge to the Cuban revolution since 1959.

The Thirtieth Anniversary of the Bay of Pigs Invasion

Fidel Castro spoke before relatives and survivors of the Bay of Pigs invasion and to members of the Cuban Communist Party on April 19, 1991 in Havana. He spoke of the similarities and differences between the attack on the revolution in 1961 and the attack on the revolution in 1991. In the first period, the Cuban defenders were young and inexperienced fighters who had little knowledge of the weapons they were carrying. The attackers assumed that they would gain control of the air, achieve victories on the ground, and would be met by Cubans on the island who had risen up against their government. None of this occurred as the young revolutionaries defended their country and defeated the U.S. sponsored attack within 72 hours. Even though the defenders were inexperienced with their weapons, they had been preparing to defend their homeland for a long time, much as the defenders of the revolution in the 1990s.

Several changes have occurred in the thirty years since the first defense of the revolution, Castro said. Cubans today had a higher level of political understanding, literacy was much greater, the Communist Party and Young Communist League were vibrant, mass organizations were healthy and the unity of the people and the people and the party was strong.

He then spoke at length about the challenges ahead for the revolution, reminding his audience that in July, 1989, he declared that the Cuban revolution would persevere even if the Socialist Bloc crumbled and the Soviet Union disintegrated in civil war. At that time, many people who heard him were puzzled by the implied prediction. By 1991, the prediction had come true. Particularly, the disintegration of the Soviet Union had made Cuba's affairs "more complicated."

The problems resulting from the end of the Socialist Bloc were many. Machinery and vehicles that were once available are no longer so. Spare parts for items produced in Eastern European countries were difficult to acquire. Trade with the Soviet Union was made complicated by the many individual enterprises the

Cubans had to deal with as opposed to central authorities in the past. Fuel supplies were more scarce and their supply was unpredictable. Similarly, scarcities in raw materials and foodstuffs were mounting. Also, imports from the Socialist Bloc came largely on Soviet merchant ships. Access to this means of transport has declined and Cuban shipping is insufficient for transporting all that was imported. Finally, the increased military threat from the United States comes at a time when military supplies are less available.

To counter the crisis, the special period had been declared and the Cuban people are working all the harder to overcome shortages and deprivations. These have included new agricultural activities to fulfill domestic food needs, the construction of dams, the development of tourism, the expansion of the export program in biotechnology and pharmaceuticals, and energy conservation measures. While all of these policies are bearing fruit, the intensity of the struggle, Castro said, was in part to be determined by the extent to which the Soviet Union disintegrated and hence reduced its traditional relationship with Cuba.

While the disintegration of the Soviet Union was a problem for Cuba, Castro argued, it was also a tragedy for much of the Third World because of the significant role the Soviets played in defending progressive countries from imperialist attack. "Today many people in the world, especially in the Third World, are realizing how important the existence of the Soviet Union was for them and how the mere existence of that country checked the United States' zeal for domination, the thirst for world domination. And it was an effective check on imperialist aggression.[13] Also after the Bolshevik Revolution and later the Cuban revolution, the imperialist powers, for pragmatic, not humanistic reasons adopted some policies to reduce the harsh conditions brought on by their exploitation. The Alliance for Progress program for Latin America was one such example.

Therefore, given the radical changes in the international system coupled with the deepening economic crisis that Third World peoples face, Cuba remains a symbol of hope for the future and an alternative to the "neoliberal" programs their leaders have been forced to adopt. These policies mean more of the same for the Third World: paying debts, privatizing economies, cutting back on government services, making economies more attractive for multinational corporations, and consequently facilitating the flow of capital from the Third World to the industrial capitalist countries.

> All of the people who still have some hope for the world, who still have progressive ideas, who dream about social justice, national dignity and independence; all of the people who dream of a better world, who detest, in one way or another, with all their heart, a world ruled by the U.S. empire and by the reactionary and fascist ideas which capitalism has engendered in this stage of its development; all those who know a bit of history, all those who have truly humane and noble ideas, concepts and values, hope that there will be resistance in the world and hope that socialism's ideas will be saved.[14]

Consequently, Fidel Castro proclaimed that through no choice of its own Cuba was assigned an historic task: "We have to defend socialism, we have to defend national independence, we have to defend our people's dignity; but we also have to defend the dreams and hopes of all the exploited peoples, all those who are humiliated and suffering in this world."[15]

I fix Typewriters for the revolution.

I am a simple country person.

I remember the bohios
and the gusanos crawling from the soil
into my older sister's bare feet
and through her body to her heart and liver
where they devoured her life
and left her on the bed staring with wide blank eyes
toward the ceiling as she died.

I remember the yuca root we ate three times a day,
the toilet on the ground among the palms
behind the bohio.
I remember how
I almost died of diarrhea when I was six
and how Lucia and Rufino the little ones did die.
I remember no electricity—ever.

I remember the sugar zafra
and how my father slept 3 hours a night
to work those few months each year
and earned $90—for the whole zafra.

I remember the fidelistas
in the mountains, the Sierra Maestra
and I heard of Fidel at bars in the village,
how everyone hoped he and his fighters
would change things
the way they said they would
when there was no more Batista.

I remember that day at the beginning of 1959
when their columns entered Habana from
Matanzas and Santa Clara,
and the war was over,
and how the people were wild,
except the owners

and
the
Americans.

I remember the Agrarian Reform,
the Urban Reform
the literacy program—
I learned how to read much better.
I remember the sabotage in the cane fields,
the blowing up of the Belgian ship "Le Coubre"
in our harbor by the CIA,
at least that's what they said—
all the mysterious explosions in those days.

And then there was Playa Giron.
I remember the school in Holguin
where I began to learn—everything.

And now—it is 30 years later.
I am older and the Yanqui strangles us
because we do not want to be owned by them.
We need everything.
It is hard.
I had potatoes and bread for the last 5 meals.
My shoes need to be fixed and I can afford it
but the shoemaker has nothing.
I get a pension and it is enough—just barely.
But we need so much
Since I am good at fixing things,
for years I fixed lamps and electric tools and typewriters.

Now I am old, much older.
But I am still useful.
I am still a revolutionary.
I fix typewriters for the revolution.

Bob Randolph

Chapter 6

Impressions of Cuba, 1990, 1991

Traveling to Cuba

I attended philosophy conferences in Havana, Cuba in 1990 and 1991 organized by the Radical Philosophy Association and other groups in the United States and hosted by the Faculty of Philosophy, History and Sociology of the University of Havana. The theme of the 1990 conference was "Human Being and Social Progress" and the 1991 conference, "The Future of Socialism: The View From Cuba." Each conference was attended by persons with a variety of interests and political perspectives. The first conference was attended by 32 scholars and professionals from several disciplines and occupations; the second by 55 persons and equally diverse.

Both conferences were framed around a schedule of tours, trips, and briefings reflecting the interests and requests of the delegations in attendance. Open time allowed for attendees to roam around Havana, engage in small meetings with Cubans representing such groups as the Cuban Women's Federation and Cuban psychologists, and to dialogue with Cuban philosophers, historians, and political scientists attending the conferences.

Marazul Travel Company secured visas from the Cuban government, organized the charter flights from Miami to Havana and back, and arranged, in conjunction with the Cuba tourist agency, hotel accommodations. Some accommodations and travel in Cuba were arranged through the University of Havana itself.

The conference hotel in which participants stayed for seven days in both years was on the outskirts of Havana and was operated by the University of Havana as a conference facility. Hotel Machurucutu was motel-like. It was surrounded by farm and cattle-grazing land with a yard and rather large hourglass-shaped pool. Down the road there was a small village. The University arranged for bus transport in 1990 into Havana at a modest cost and the same service was provided the next year so that the U.S. delegates could use off hours to explore the city and engage in random dialogue with Cuban citizens.

Both before and after the conferences, the U.S. delegation stayed in hotels in downtown Havana. In the two years attending the conferences, I stayed in four different hotels, each in convenient locations to historic and tourist sites in the city. In both the conference and non-conference hotels, meals were provided.

Cubaturs and the University of Havana provided bus and tour service to a variety of locations of interest to our groups. These included the University of Havana, a women's prison, a psychiatric institute, an accelerated science-oriented high school, a cigar factory, an agricultural cooperative, the Museum of the Revolution, the Hemingway museum, a four-year language university, and the famous Veradero Beach. The delegation also received briefings on Cuba from a variety of experts: Karen Wald, a U.S. journalist; Marc Frank, a U.S. journalist; Carlos Tablada, a Cuban economist, and staff members of the international affairs division of the Cuban Communist Party. A team of five translators from the language university were also a constant source of information about Cuba. Finally, several Cuban scholars presented papers and led discussions on issues related to Cuba's role in the international system and U.S./Cuban relations.

It is important to note that the philosophers, social scientists, and others attending the 1990 and 1991 conferences represented a rather exclusive group of U.S. citizens in that with the exception of a short period from 1977 to 1982, the United States has prohibited its citizens from visiting Cuba as tourists. Only narrowly defined categorizes of U.S. citizens can travel to Cuba: researchers and journalists with a professional interest in Cuba, and Cuban-Americans. Persons who travel to Cuba as tourists may be prosecuted and subjected to a large fine and jail sentence.

This prohibition was put in place in the 1960s and reestablished by President Reagan to limit Cuba's access to dollars while people from Europe, Canada, and Latin America are increasingly visiting Cuba to enjoy its beautiful beaches, fascinating culture, relatively developed tourist infrastructure, lack of violence and drugs, and inexpensive lodging and food. Despite the ban on travel, the daily charter flight each day between Cuba and Miami is usually full, mostly with Cuban-Americans visiting their relatives and homeland. While the Cuban government on occasion exercises its prerogative to deny visas to U.S. citizens, for Cubans who had emigrated, the limitations on travel are largely the result of U.S. policy, not Cuban policy.

The University of Havana and Old Havana

The historical context for our 1990 conference was set by a press release received by the delegates from the Cuban Interest Section in Washington a week before our departure. The communique, dated April 29, 1990, was entitled "U.S. Conducts Large Military Maneuvers Aimed at Cuba." The document described the beginnings of larger than usual U.S. military maneuvers in the Caribbean, thousands of troops and air and sea exercises, with a clear targeting of simulated battle actions against Cuba. The activities included an evacuation of U.S. civilians from Guantanamo.

The document argued that with the demise of the Warsaw Pact, the change of government in Nicaragua, the new "docile and submissive" government put in place in Panama, the exercises had no strategic justification. For the Cubans, the only logical assumption that could be made was that the U.S. was practicing for a military assault on Cuba, one of the last bastions of opposition to U.S. world hegemony.

The press release sent personally to the U.S. delegation was probably the first most of us had heard of the exercises, as they received virtually no coverage in the media. Cubans, however, were made aware of this threat to their sovereignty and, because of the clear possibility that the simulations could become reality, the island was put on alert and the army and civilian militia were mobilized to deter any potential attack. Ironically, one of our translators told several of us at a party that we were courageous to come to Cuba at this time of great tension. Therefore, the continued U.S. hostilities to the Cuban revolution provided the ongoing context for our visit, and a critical undercurrent of all our dialogue, investigation, and site visits was concern on the part of Cubans and North Americans about how to change this thirty-year policy of hostility and aggression.

Such high-minded political questions were dwarfed on the first days of our trip to Cuba in 1990 by the more mundane activities of getting there and our initial impressions of the physical and human landscape of the country. As to the former, we flew an Air Haiti charter packed with about 150 Cuban-Americans and the thirty U.S. conference delegates. The 1990 flight was late at night, the 1991 flight during the peak late morning flying time. Some commentators claimed that the U.S. government required a change in flight times to force the charter service to increase its charge and hence make it more expensive for U.S. citizens to travel to Cuba.

Upon arrival at about midnight, on the first trip, we were whisked through Cuban customs by a guide from Cubaturs, who would also be our guide the first and second weekends of the trip. We were bused to Hotel Presidente and quickly placed in rooms. The word spread that this was the hotel occupied by U.S. gangster, Meyer Lansky, in the 1950s. I felt personally assured that the accommodations would thus be more than adequate, which turned out to be true on both trips.

The following morning of our first trip, and the second one as well, we were taken to the University of Havana for a welcoming and a walking tour of the University. We met the Dean of the College of Philosophy and History, the head of the Institute for the Study of Philosophy, and others from the University and government. We were encouraged to list places in and around Havana we would like to see, persons we would like to meet from organizations. It was made clear that as far as resources and time would allow, the University organizers of the conference would accommodate as many requests as possible.

As we were escorted around campus we learned that the University had its roots in the 18th century and is at its current location, in the center of Havana just blocks from the "downtown" area, since the turn of the 20th century. General Leonard Wood, U.S. occupying officer in the aftermath of the "Spanish American" War (the Cubans argue that the title of the war should include "Cuban"), constructed the new campus as a replica of Columbia University, his alma mater.

On the site we visited the University has a variety of faculties, primarily in the humanities, social sciences, and law, with other campus sites spread around the city. About 18,000 students attend the University of Havana and are taught by 1,000 faculty. There are several other universities in each of the fourteen provinces of the country. The professor of Roman law who guided our visit in 1990 described in rich detail the significance and historic references of buildings and murals and pridefully illustrated to us that he could speak in five languages including Latin and Hebrew. While not "political" in the traditional sense, he pointed out the tank in the central quadrangle of the university, which he said was a gift from the Eisenhowers to Batista. This tank was part of the armament stockpile used against the revolutionaries struggling to oust Batista. The law professor noted that the tank's gun was pointed at the building of the Rector of the University. He wryly indicated that now it could be put to a useful purpose.

Our 1991 tour was led by a woman whose specialty was history, but not necessarily that of the University. She gave us a more "political" tour, visiting a small meeting room that had photos of student martyrs to the revolutionary struggles against the Machado dictatorship in the 1920s and the Batista dictatorship in the 1950s. She made it clear that students played leading roles in these efforts and students were instrumental in the formation of the Cuban Communist Party and a variety of other revolutionary formations that so shaped twentieth century Cuba. Fidel Castro, as with many students at the University of Havana, was a political activist while he studied law in the 1940s.

On the first Saturday of both trips, after visiting the University, we were escorted on walking tours of Old Havana — in process of restoration with support from the United Nations and the Cuban government. Old Havana was established in 1519 as the capital of Spanish colonialism in the new world. Spanish traffickers in gold, jewels, and certain foodstuffs disembarked at Havana on the way to Spanish colonies in Latin America and similarly stopped on the way back to Spain with goods appropriated from the continent. Those staying in Havana built the magnificent city that has been an attraction to tourists and scholars of Spanish colonialism and Cuban history.

Old Havana consists of some 900 buildings of historical significance including forts, churches, palaces, and residences. Walking the small winding streets, one is reminded of similar architectural wonders in Madrid, Paris, or Rome. On one square surrounded by a variety of buildings including an old church, some craftspersons sold their wares and a band played rhumba music. A crowd of observers saw a very old man engaged in Cuba's national dance, the rhumba, proud as could be of his dancing skills and the audience he had assembled.

The 1990 delegation was taken on a boat ride across the bay in a replica of a 17th century Spanish vessel to the Morro Castle. The Morro Castle was built by the Spanish in the 18th century to protect the access to Havana from pirates and the British, who had occupied Havana in 1762. After climbing 150 steps to the castle, we had a gorgeous view of the entire city of Havana across the bay. Shortly before 9 p.m., a squad of soldiers dressed in old Spanish uniforms marched to an old cannon and at precisely nine, the cannon was fired. Every night this cannon is fired and Havana residents are known to set their clocks by it.

This first day's experience on both visits seemed contradictory to the press release about the U.S. maneuvers and the political motivation for our visit. Cuba, to North Americans, is framed in Cold War terms by both those who agree *and* who disagree with U.S. foreign policy. The Cuba we were experiencing was a country with a rich history, a beautiful architecture, a profound cultural pride, and a tourist sensibility about what foreigners might be most interested in concerning their country. In these ways, Cuba did not seem very different from other countries, including the United States.

Havana, The New City

The first morning of my first visit to Havana, several of us were up early and walked the two blocks from the Hotel Presidente to the sea and looked back across the Havana skyline. Later in the day we were bused to the University and to Old Havana. My first reaction was that Havana was a city of beauty and cleanliness and yet full of activity, people and car traffic, although *very* modest by U.S. urban standards.

Something about Havana seemed different to me than my home town, Chicago, or New York, or Indianapolis. Finally I realized what it was. There were no commercial signs, billboards or other symbols of capitalism. This was a city without overt commercialism. Reflecting further, Havana did not have overabundant political posters and billboards either. In fact, I saw more billboards, signs, and murals exhorting people to support the revolution in Managua in 1987 than I saw in Havana on my two visits. Of course, there were some signs with slogans, drawings of Che in various locations, and there was the multi-storied mural of Che adjacent to the Plaza of the Revolution on a government building. But despite these, Havana was a city without advertising. For U.S. journalists this illustrated Havana's "gray" or "Stalin-like" character. For me, the lack of advertising made the city even more beautiful, blending into the natural environment of sea and landscape.

Traffic was light. A majority of cars were Soviet Ladas, small boxy vehicles. However, there were a large number of vintage U.S. automobiles from the 1940s and 1950s; Chevys, Oldsmobiles, Fords, Buicks. Cubans who owned these reworked them and kept them running, since access to new American cars was prohibited by the U.S. embargo. The site of all these old vehicles led one of our delegates to burst out after we had cleared customs: "My God, I feel that we've gone back in time to my teenage years."

There was one significant change that I noted in 1991. In 1991 Cuba began to face a severe shortage of oil because of the failure of the Soviet Union to deliver oil contracted for in recent trade agreements. The Cuban government, therefore, had to impose severe rationing of energy resources. Public transportation was cut, tractor use was reduced and farmers returned to plowing and harvesting with pack animals, and even factories and construction projects were cut back to conserve energy.

The only good news about the enormous hardships imposed by the energy shortage was the introduction of bicycles as a major mode of transportation. In addition to the bicycles imported from China, the Cubans have begun to assemble their own. Consequently, where only a handful of bicycles were seen in 1990, they were pervasive in 1991.

Not only is this a constructive energy-saving policy with positive health consequences (except for the large increase in accidents), the speedy adaptation illustrates the flexible and experimental nature of the Cuban political economy and social structure. It is this adaptability that has been the hallmark of the revolutionary regime since 1959.

Our travels around Havana in 1990 and 1991 were limited to some degree, but everywhere we went we saw attractive housing units, usually multiple-storied apartment complexes, some old, some relatively new. Cubans pay no more than six percent of their salaries for rent and after a period of years are entitled to claim ownership of their living quarters.

Cubans seemed to live in housing units all around the city with no distinctions made as to their location in relation to the city center or the area where diplomatic missions are located. One of our translators, a professor at the Pedagogical Institute, lived with his family about five blocks from the "downtown" area where the famous ice cream-laden Coppelia Park could be found and the glamorous Havana Libre. When our translator showed us his parents' apartment, old but elegant in its large and high-ceilinged rooms, I thought that in Chicago this apartment would be a high priced condominium demanding a premium price because of its location.

While every Cuban, and every Havana resident is housed—in two visits I saw only one drunk rifling through garbage cans and no homeless people—everyone spoke of a serious housing shortage such that many family members must live together in rather small housing units. We heard of apocryphal cases where young couples living with one set of parents decided to get a divorce but, because of the housing shortage, had to continue to live together until such time as new housing became available. Before the "special period" of economic austerity was brought about by the changes in Eastern Europe, the Cubans had begun to construct new housing and public buildings using the rubric of the microbrigades, groups of neighborhood residents who volunteer to construct their own buildings. The microbrigades had constructed much housing in the early 1970s, but the activity was dropped until the 1986 Rectification campaign rekindled the spirit of volunteerism.

Cuba was well developed even before the revolution compared with many Latin American countries. Most of the hotels in Havana that were used by U.S. tourists in the 1940s and 1950s are still operational. The Havana Libre, formerly the Havana Hilton, is at the center of tourist life and the city proper.

Consequently the center city is dotted with large hotels, easy access to Old Havana and the lovely central park, Coppelia. Well-kept museums display Cuban art and history, and the presence in the 1930s and 1940s of Ernest Hemingway. Old and New Havana provide an ideal mix of an old European-style city with modern tourist attractions. Thus while the revolution wiped out the gambling and prostitution, it left intact the tourist infrastructure that is a key element of Cuba's hope for economic survival in the years ahead. Given Cuba's natural beauty, its existent tourist infrastructure, the lack of violence, prostitution and drugs, and modest travel costs, Cuba would quickly become a major tourist attraction to U.S. citizens if the government ended the prohibition on travel.

Varadero Beach and the Contradictions of Tourism

Cuba has some of the most beautiful beaches in the Caribbean and is in the process of readying more for the hoped-for tourist boom. The preeminent location is the famous Varadero Beach, located in Matanzas province, about 150 miles east of Havana. On the Sunday of both trips we were bused to Varadero Beach for a day's frolicking in the sun before the academic work of the conferences began on Monday.

The drive to the beach gave us a fascinating glimpse of the Cuban countryside, dotted with housing projects adjacent to factories and occasional drilling rigs optimistically pumping for oil. We saw construction near completion for housing and athletic structures for the Pan American games. We passed the Jose Martí Pioneer village, which usually serves as a campsite for Cuban children in the summers. It was currently used to house some 250 children from the Soviet Union, victims of the Chernobyl nuclear plant disaster. Further along on our trip we viewed a large housing project called Alamar, constructed by workers in the early 1970s to house some 400 families, most of whom were involved in the construction. Closer to the beach we drove through the city of Matanzas, with a 100,000 population and a university serving 10, 000 students.

The splendor of the gentle rolling hills and rich green valleys viewed through one side of the bus was matched by images of the sea and undamaged shorelines on the other. Along the way we saw sisal fields, groves of mango trees, banana plantations, and grazing livestock. The highway from Havana to Varadero, paved and in excellent condition, was sparsely used, perhaps illustrating the impact of the austerity program due to fuel shortages. On the second trip, we even noted an occasional bicyclist chugging along the highway.

At the beach, we were on our own to sun and swim or hide in the shade of thatched awnings sipping beer or Cuban rum. Most of the delegates did some of each as we became acquainted: where we had come from, what we studied, why we were in Cuba, was it our first time or one of many visits. The majority of delegates were visiting Cuba for the first time. Some had made several trips, particularly the conference organizers and group leaders. A few had been to Cuba either before the revolution or in the 1960s.

One delegate to the second conference, poet Bob Randolph, had been to Cuba in the early days of the revolution and returned to see what the last thirty years had brought to the Cuban people and to write about it. Over the next two weeks, he wrote poems about what he saw and heard and also how Cuban life was affected by U.S. foreign policy.

On the first visit, lunch was provided in the luxurious Internacional Hotel. We had our choice of food from a sumptuous spread, including beef, chicken, vegetables, fried plantains, breads, and various cakes for dessert. The Cuban specialty, citrus fruits and drinks, was in abundance. Ironically, many of the delegates could not have afforded to experience this much luxury during a usual vacation. On our second visit, we were placed in a beach site between hotels and had to purchase more modest food, although our hosts from the University of Havana did provide canned beer.

The Varadero Beach experience pointed out to us the contradictions of life in Cuba. While it is true that workers are able to enjoy vacations, and to holiday on beaches and in resorts like Varadero, the tourism industry requires that foreign guests receive special services, accommodations, foods, and drink not available to the average Cuban. In a highly competitive international industry, tourist entrepreneurs must provide the best in these tourist commodities *and* also have the physical space to meet tourist demands. Tourist attractiveness is one of the "comparative advantages" countries like Cuba have in international economic terms. With the collapse of the Soviet Bloc, Cuba is forced to return to its tourist past to earn desperately needed foreign exchange.

Paradoxically, therefore, to defend the Cuban Revolution from collapse, it must adopt an economic strategy that in many ways contradicts the values of the revolution. Cubans are prohibited from various tourist areas, particularly hotels. Cubans cannot buy goods in the dollar stores in hotels. Cubans do not have access to the varieties and quantities of food that are available to tourists. Cubans are finding ever shorter supplies of electricity, water, fuel, and public transportation while these basics must be available to tourists if they are to choose Cuba for their vacations. In other words, in the heart of a society that stands more for ending privilege than virtually any other society in the world, the Cubans have been forced to provide that privilege for foreign visitors to save the revolution.

Tourism is also a contradictory economic activity in that it generates among some host country citizens a false sense of economic possibilities. One of the extraordinary political tools used by international capitalism over the last twenty years has been the ever more concentrated instruments of mass media and popular culture. From news to television entertainment to film to reading material, the world's citizens have been bombarded with the image of gluttonous mass consumption guaranteed to those who choose capitalist societies. Even those self-reflective and appreciative of the gains achieved in health care, free education, housing and other fundamental rights of a revolutionary society fall prey to the expectation that along with these gains, capitalist societies also offer video recorders, fancy cars, and other products of late capitalism.

Tourists are the second most important bearers of the images of consumerism to reach Cuban society, surpassed only by the global media empires. Further, intrinsic to being a tourist is the assumption that the high mass consumption life style can be experienced within the tourist country itself. Consequently Cubans see their daily struggles in stark comparison with the hyperbolic images of consumerism represented by the visitors to their country.

A final way in which Cuban tourism is contradictory has to do with foreign investment. The Cubans, strapped for foreign exchange and the resources to complete construction projects begun before the international crisis, now must encourage foreign investment. To become attractive to foreign investors, Cuba must be seen as having potential for profitmaking. This clearly is the case for tourism and Cuban tourism has attracted investors from Spain, Germany, Great Britain, and Canada. To encourage this investment, however, the Cubans have had to allow foreigners to manage their investments and to allow labor/management relations that are acceptable to the investors. Of course, central to the Marxist understanding of imperialism is the presupposition that capitalist penetration is exploitative and contrary to the principles of the revolution. Therefore tourism, and other forms of investment curried by the government, has required the freeing of foreign capital operating in Cuba, in contradiction to the goals of revolution.

Some of the contradictory character of Cuban life was reflected in a pleasant talk I had with a worker in 1991 on the beach. In the early afternoon, I meandered away from my beachfront thatched shelter to take a walk. A Cuban man, perhaps in his fifties, stopped me to talk. I appreciated his outgoing nature in that I am not usually an outgoing person and therefore would be less likely to have random dialogue with Cubans on the street. The man spoke to me in excellent English. In fact, he stopped me because he loved to speak English. A long time ago he decided he wanted to learn the language. He believed that intelligence and education were important. He showed me an English grammar and translation book that he was carrying in a plastic bag in order to study in his spare time.

My friend said that the Cuban economy was hurting. Cubans had enough money but no goods to purchase. He could not get razor blades, or toys for his grandchildren. He said that Cubans and the United States should get along better, particularly now that the Cuban relationship with the Soviet Union had changed. He used an analogy in which a man is hit by a truck and when he gets up he asks the truck driver for help. Continuing, my friend said that Fidel was very intelligent but had made mistakes. Varadero could have had 100 more hotels except for errors. Also he indicated that Cubans in the past were not allowed to speak with tourists. He obviously felt no constraints in our discussion.

In general, I could not discern what his politics were although he did relate to me that health care, education, and other valuables were free and that his son was able to get an education under the regime and was an engineer. I surmised that my friend was proud of his country and its revolution but was concerned about the radical shift in Cuba's fortunes and was critical of several government policies. I sensed he was a man who thoughtfully and critically reflected on his place in Cuban society.

Viewing Cuban Institutions

During our two visits, the agenda was set based upon delegate requests and the feasibility of visits determined by our hosts. Of course, we recognized, and our hosts at these various sites made it clear, that most of those places we went were selected by the government for foreigners to visit. In some visits we were allowed to move freely and talk with any Cubans we saw. In other visits, such as the women's prison, our activities were limited to the guided tour and a question and answer session with the director of the prison. At the prison, no photographs were allowed.

One afternoon after the close of the philosophy conference in 1990, we were led by our Cubatur guide to the Jose Martí Cigar Factory formerly known as the H. Upmann Company. This old four-story building some six blocks from our hotel housed 654 workers, who produced high quality cigars in a highly labor intensive manufacturing process.

Upon entering the factory, the visitor could not help but notice the large portrait painting of an Afro-Cuban man who was a founder of the cigar workers union in Cuba. After meeting the factory manager and the factory union leader, both Afro-Cuban women, we proceeded through the factory floor by floor. On the lowest level, workers were seated in circles unraveling huge tobacco leaves and setting them out for further processing. As we moved upstairs to the second, third, and fourth floors we observed the transformation of these leaves into tightly packed cigars with ringlike labels on each and finally expertly placed in wooden cigar boxes with cigars exactly the same shade of brown.

Sixty percent of the workforce in this cigar factory were Afro-Cuban, whose average salary was 163 pesos a month. The national average was 192 pesos and the salary range in Cuba was from 100 to 400 pesos for workers. Seventy percent of the workers at the cigar factory were women. The workers were on the shop floor six and one half hours, had an hour for lunch and two

fifteen minute breaks. Lunches were provided for 30 to 50 cen-
tavos. A doctor was on staff at the factory and had training in
occupational diseases most common to cigar workers. Pregnant
women were moved to physically easier jobs in the factory and
received one and one half months paid maternity leave before
and after the birth of a child. Jobs were held for new mothers for
one year. Workers retired at age 55, and those completing 25
years of service were entitled to retirement wages at fifty percent
of their working salaries.

Each floor of the factory had its own union local and one trade
union bureau spoke for the workers in the entire factory. Union
locals met monthly and union leaders met with factory management once a year to discuss quality control, workplace and other
issues.

Only one section of the factory was air-conditioned, where
cigars were boxed, so the building was relatively hot and stuffy.
Fans were operating throughout the factory and despite the heat
and humidity, the factory floors were light and airy. Workers,
while having production quotas, seemed relaxed and worked at a
steady but not breakneck speed. In the tradition of cigar workers
in Cuba and the United States, these workers were read to from
newspapers and books in the mornings and afternoons from a
platform, with a microphone, to help satisfy the intellectual curi-
osity of the workers. When we arrived on the third floor where
some two hundred workers were rolling cigars, we were taken to
the platform where the readings occurred. We were introduced
and in unison the workers, with smiles on their faces, clanked
their cigar rolling tools, making a loud tinny sound. This was the
customary welcome to visitors.

We also visited an agricultural cooperative, formerly two that
had merged: one had been named after a martyr from the Vietnam War, the other named after Augusto Sandino, the Nicara-
guan hero of the 1930s. This cooperative, comprising about 1,000
acres, had 138 members, 14 women, and had been in existence
for nine years. The cooperative produced foodstuffs for domestic
consumption such as garlic, sweet potatoes, onions, beans, and
tomatoes. Also chickens and rabbits were bred. Part of the land
was used for production for cooperative members and the rest to
grow produce for sale to the state.

Most co-op members lived in Havana but new housing for them was under construction in the neighboring town, San Antonio los Español. Before the revolution farmers had small plots of land, if any, and lived in scattered locations around the countryside. Those who did not work on state farms after the revolution were encouraged to form cooperatives to more efficiently produce on larger landholdings and to bring disparate peoples together to more easily provide public services such as health care and education, and to make available farm equipment and fertilizers. About 38 percent of Cuban farming was "private," but much of this included farmers in cooperatives.

The cooperative is governed by a political and an administrative branch selected from the membership. Of the total income, fifty percent goes to individual members and the other share is divided into investment, education and recreation, and the general fund of the cooperative. Cooperative members work ten hour days and earn about 4,500 pesos per year. Members get a one-month vacation. Some are able to vacation at the beach.

The Augusto Sandino Cooperative was the site of our voluntary labor, a symbolic demonstration of solidarity with the workers and peasants of Cuba. Or this was what we were told. Consequently, we all dressed for the hot sweaty work that we expected. After the initial briefing in the meeting hall we were taken outside and offered sandwiches and beer (at 10:30 a.m.). Then we were taken to bean fields. Here, we assumed, the arduous work would begin. About three of our delegation were invited to pick a few beans. They then passed them around for some others to nibble on. After this manifestation of North American labor, we were urged back on the buses and our voluntary labor was over.

In 1990 several of our delegation traveled an hour by bus from Havana to visit the Lenin School, a senior high school organized to instruct high achieving tenth, eleventh, and twelfth grade mathematics and science students. The six classes or divisions of students alternated being available to meet with visitors so as to spread the burden of constant visitations. The Lenin School, the first of such special schools, one for each of Cuba's fourteen provinces, was founded in January, 1974. The enrollment at this school was 3,774 students; 62 percent were young women.

The curricula resembled that of other high schools in Cuba except that students received accelerated instruction in mathematics and science, including biology, physics, chemistry, and electronics. Despite the science emphasis, students did receive instruction in languages, social sciences, history, as well as in art, theatre, music, and dance. Among the distinguishing features of the academic program was that students were initiated into advanced scientific study through seminars and research. They were encouraged to be active participants in the educational process as evidenced by the scientific museum created and maintained by the students.

The curriculum was very demanding. Students studied and attended classes for ten hours a day. They also performed two hours of physical education per day and up to three hours of optional sports. Along with class, study, and sporting activities, students assumed primary responsibility for cleaning and maintaining the school complex, a multi-building assortment of classrooms, dormitories, physical education facilities, and faculty housing units much like a college campus. Finally, students spend 3 1/2 hours a week on vegetable gardening. The principal of the school indicated that educational policy was to create well-rounded women and men who appreciated and experienced physical labor as well as intellectual labor.

The principal noted that education in Cuba was free. This included transportation and boarding of students. They lived at school during the week and returned home during weekends. Parents' councils periodically interacted with the staff of the school and the principal emphasized that the home environment and support of parents reinforced the in-school experience; parent input into the educational process was of significant import to its overall success.

Students were chosen to attend the Lenin School as a result of high achievement in mathematics and Spanish exams and outstanding grades earned in junior high school. The Lenin School serviced students from La Habana province and the Isle of Youth. Quotas insured that there was equitable representation of students from rural areas. In the 1989-1990 academic year 1,400 new students were admitted. Two thousand of some 4,600 applicants had been admitted for the 1990-1991 year. Ninety-one to 95 percent of the students graduating from the Lenin School each year attended the university.

Of the 14 special science schools, each had a different architecture based upon the aesthetics of the architect, input from the educational staff, and the available resources. The Lenin School was a complex of several buildings set in a lush rural environment. The classroom buildings were open, airy, and cool despite the Cuban heat and humidity. Artistic works on walls and in corridors were prepared by the students. It was a beautiful educational setting, comparable to the loveliest of university campuses in the U.S.

One of the teachers proudly reported that students from the Lenin School had participated in an international mathematics contest in 1980. The Cuban team placed second and one student won a first place award. In 1986, the contest was held at the Lenin School. Along with demonstrated mathematics skills, each student at the school was computer literate and had access to a computer. As we were told about the students' achievements, a computer musical rendition of "We Are the World" played over the loud speaker to signal the end of one class period.

While the Lenin School was a model institution, one that Cubans were proud to show visitors, it clearly illustrated the pedagogical principles that undergird the Cuban vision of a successful educational process. Students actively and rigorously participate in a rich educational experience that mixed science, the arts, physical education, and manual labor in an architectural and natural setting that was healthful and aesthetically appealing.

The 1990 delegation had the interesting experience of visiting a maximum security women's prison. Most of us had little familiarity with U.S. prisons but we found this particular prison, its physical facilities, its staff, and its policies to be enlightening, compared to what little we knew of U.S. prisons. This prison sought to rehabilitate the inmates.

The prison was constructed in 1982 and could house 1,000 prisoners although only 300 were incarcerated when we visited. Most inmates, ages ranging from their twenties to their sixties and averaging thirty years of age, were jailed for stealing and so-called "passionate crimes"; that is, killing their husbands. Inmates slept in beautifully decorated rooms, housing six inmates per unit. Rooms were available for family visits, which occurred every two weeks with conjugal visits allowed every three weeks. Other rooms were available for inmate visits with their lawyers.

Also, there was a well-stocked library and a small theatre with a stage for inmate performances. Finally, there was a 26-bed hospital. As to medical care, a doctor was on permanent staff and inmates received vaccinations and physical examinations on a regular basis.

Inmates worked a 40-hour week with Saturdays and Sundays off, earning a wage that could be saved or sent to families. Most prisoners worked in textile manufacturing in open and airy rooms (a better work environment than the cigar factory) and some prisoners who completed their sentence continued to work in the textile factory.

It was clear that prison policy was to rehabilitate prisoners and to assist their reentry into community life. Along with the factory work experience, inmates received classes in embroidery and other skills that could be useful after their sentences were completed. A literary club met in the library every week and those so inclined were encouraged to write poetry and fiction. Upon release, representatives of the Federation of Cuban Women and the Committee for the Defense of the Revolution in the community where the ex-prisoner will reside aid in their reacculturation into the community, urging fellow citizens to overcome their prejudices against convicted felons. One byproduct of these efforts was a low recidivism rate.

During the two conferences, delegates observed these and a variety of other Cuban institutions. Some visited a biotechnology plant, a psychiatric institute, the sites for the Pan-American games, a philosophy institute, a neighborhood organization, and several museums including the Museum of the Revolution, a museum of contemporary art, and the Ernest Hemingway house. All these visits reinforced our sense that the Cuban revolution remained committed to improving the quality of life of the Cuban people, to stimulating economic development, and to engaging in substantial self-criticism and social experimentation. The visits to the cigar factory, the agricultural cooperative, the accelerated high school, and the women's prison convinced us then, if we had not been convinced earlier, that the Cuban revolution was a precious social laboratory that needed to be supported and encouraged, not attacked.

Briefings By U.S. Citizens Working in Cuba

During our two conference visits we received several briefings which turned out to be two- to five-hour discussions of Cuba's history, problems, and future. Two briefings were with North American journalists living in Cuba; Marc Frank, who wrote for the *People's Weekly World*, and Karen Wald who wrote for *The Guardian, Z,* and other U.S. and European publications. Both had lived in Cuba for several years. Frank spoke to us in May, 1990 and Wald in May, 1990 and June 1991.

Mark Frank began his two-hour session with a discussion of what the Cubans call their "rectification" campaign. The rectification campaign, at the time of our briefing in 1990, was in its fifth year and was scheduled to be the central subject of the Fourth Congress of the Cuban Communist Party in October 1991.

To Frank, rectification was the process of evaluating and acting toward the solution of social, economic, and political problems existent in the revolutionary process. Emphasis was on problem solving, drawing much more fully than in the 1970s on mass participation. The first instance of rectification, Frank claimed, was noted in the new Cuban defense program begun in 1981. At that time, the Reagan Administration had made it clear that U.S./Cuban relations were going to worsen. Cuba had relied on its professional army for defense, and the military, as other institutions, had become bureaucratized and distant from the Cuban people. Consequently, the government began a program to mobilize the Cuban people to participate in their own defense. This involved teaching three million Cubans to shoot machineguns and to encourage them to participate in a massive tree-planting campaign to create shelter from attack.

In November, 1984, party and government leaders had an emergency meeting to evaluate the impact of ongoing policies of investment on international economic relations. While official reported economic growth rates were high in the first part of the 1980s, 7.5 percent increase in gross national product per annum, there was a belief that figures were based upon exaggerated reports and that competition between economic sectors was inhibiting rational allocations of resources. As a result a special planning group was established at the Third Party Congress begun in February, 1986. The Congress then adjourned and reassembled late in the year.

In the interim between the start of the Party Congress and the resumption of it, intense self-critical discussions occurred around the country, concerning a variety of issue areas including mounting economic problems, health care delivery, and education. From this, rectification became institutionalized. Efforts were made to increase the level of mass participation in all phases of Cuban life.

Many changes occurred over the next several years. Cubans developed a system of centralized investment to increase export earnings, and plans for import substitutions. Construction projects based on voluntary labor expanded dramatically. Efforts were made to improve labor/management relations. A new program of "continuous planning" was institutionalized, whereby workers were to be involved in planning decisions at the factory level on an ongoing basis rather than only once a year. Principles of cost accounting were instituted.

Cubans began to produce bulldozers and railroad cars as part of their import substitution strategy. New housing *and* public building construction expanded dramatically. Forty-five thousand Havana residents joined microbrigades to build new housing or renovate old neighborhoods. Between 1987 and 1990, 54 new daycare centers were constructed. Community residents were given construction tools and supplies. Those with jobs outside the home were given leave and all microbrigade workers received salaries. The housing units constructed were occupied by those who built them.

Typical microbrigades consisted of 17 people, often run by women who worked in the home. The microbrigade movement had offered women the opportunity to gain construction skills and to assume positions of leadership at the local level.

The microbrigade movement served also to reintegrate into society young persons convicted of juvenile delinquency and aided the return of those convicted of crimes. Most critically, microbrigades were helping Cubans deal with their severe housing shortage and the renovation of slum neighborhoods.

Frank argued that the rectification program constituted a significant effort to rekindle the revolutionary spirit, but he emphasized that the changes being carried out were not based upon panic and chaos, nor were they very rapid. He seemed to be suggesting that these changes were *not* the same as those that had been occurring in Eastern Europe and the Soviet Union from 1985 to 1990. Rather they reflected the general spirit of the thirty-year revolution, a spirit of experimentation, commitment to change, and self-criticism.

While the rectification campaign had its own internal dynamic, Frank did agree that such changes were occurring in a broad historical and global context. He reported that 88 percent of Cuba's trade and aid had come from Eastern Europe and the Soviet Union, with 70 coming from the Soviet Union alone. Even at the time he was speaking to us, the Eastern European countries had reneged on their long-standing trade agreements and were demanding new arrangements, primarily that all trade be carried out with hard currencies. However, at the time of our briefing in May, 1990, the Soviet Union and Cuba had signed a new, and the largest trade agreement in the history of their relationship.

Despite the new trade pact with the Soviet Union, Cubans in 1990 were already discussing what they would do if the Soviet regime collapsed. Cubans were aware that the Soviets faced severe economic problems and Castro had indicated that a civil war in the Soviet Union was possible. Frank also noted that there were strong political pressures within the Soviet Union to cut ties to Cuba.

Another element in the economic analysis that was raised by Frank had to do with tourism. It was a growth sector of the economy. Travel to Cuba was popular among foreigners because a Cuban vacation could be family oriented and safe. The government had plans for expanding the industry until the year 2,000, and at the time of the briefing, tours to Cuba were completely booked.

Frank responded to questions about Cuban politics and society. Corruption among leaders was minimal, he said. As to human rights, from 1988 to 1990, about 20 or 30 arrests were made that had connotations of human rights violations. Frank believed that those vulnerable to political arrests were usually those Cubans with ties to the U.S. interest section. There was a correlation between increasing U.S. acts of aggression and increases in Cuban repression. Dissidents in 1990 constituted a tiny minority of the population and they tended to be used by the United States. As to general political discourse, Cubans tended to be reserved at

official gatherings but informally and with each other said what
they pleased.

The rationing system guaranteed every Cuban a basic mini-
mum diet. Every child got one bottle of milk a day. Quantities of
food in the ration system were modest. As a result of Soviet/Cu-
ban agreements, Soviet technicians were allowed larger rations
than the average Cuban. These higher rations were allocated also
to all internationalists living in Cuba. In general Frank said life
was not easy for Cubans. They were industrious and they worked
long and hard. In many respects Cuba was like a Third World
country; in others Cuba was like a developed country.

As to social problems, juvenile delinquency and petty theft
existed. Child abuse was infrequent. The kidnapping of children
did not occur. Alcoholism was a problem of modest proportions.
Party and government officials had been emphasizing the need to
strengthen the family to overcome youth problems. It was believed that delinquency was often a function of parents not having adequate time for their children because of work, volunteer
labor, and political activity.

Cuba had established a national commission to coordinate the
activities of various social agencies to solve some of these problems. For example, several organizations could have some role to
play in dealing with juvenile delinquency. The national commission encourages all such organizations to work together on the
issue. This coordinated effort then was reproduced at the provincial and local levels as well. To illustrate he took the case of a
Cuban released from jail. Representatives of the trade union, the
Committee for the Defense of the Revolution, and local Party
activists would work together to ease the individual's reintegra-
tion into the community.

Frank also discussed Cuban health care and AIDS. He said that
Cubans define every health problem as a major struggle that
required the full resources of the society for its solution. The
response to the AIDS threat was "typically Cuban." They invented
a new blood-testing machine (now exported) that could process
large numbers of patients more quickly. Millions of Cubans had
been tested for AIDS. They established a sanitarium for AIDS
patients that was a beautiful facility. AIDS patients, at first quar-
antined, could return home on weekends with an escort (Wald
pointed out that this policy of escorting and restricting mobility

of AIDS patients was being changed). As a result of this national campaign, the rate of incidence of the disease was low.

Frank was asked about the U.S. threat and leadership transition in Cuba. As to the first, he claimed that the threat of U.S. invasion was always a reality. Many critics of U.S. policy had been sure that the U.S. would not invade Panama. Also the military threat did force Cubans to spend scarce resources on defense and the threat further served to deter some foreigners from touring Cuba.

As to leadership transition, Frank said that Cubans had been blessed and cursed by having one of the great leaders of the 20th century. There was no question that when Fidel Castro leaves the scene, the loss would be enormous and the consequences great. However, the revolution was many people. It had been institutionalized. Fidel Castro did not make all the decisions, nor did he do all the work. So far, Frank concluded, the revolution was the Cuban people.

As with many of her generation, Karen Wald identified strongly with the revolutionary heroism of Fidel Castro and Che Guevara. She started coming to Cuba in 1969 and in 1973 wrote her first book on Cuba called *Children of Che*. Later, while living in Oakland, California with her mischievous son, she came to the realization that this obstreperous child would not survive on the rough streets of that city. Consequently she moved to Cuba where he could not fall prey to drugs, crime, violence, and police brutality.

Wald spoke to delegations for endless hours in 1990 and 1991, clearly demonstrating her breadth of knowledge, fascination, and enthusiasm about the Cuban experiment. She provided the delegates with an opportunity to ask a variety of questions about Cuba that had not been addressed in briefings, tours, and interactions at the conferences.

In 1990 questions dealt extensively with how the Cuban economy worked and what were its problems. For example, delegates at the 1990 conference were puzzled about the existence of a variety of high priced luxury goods, such as refrigerators, in store windows in central Havana. Who purchased these goods and how could they be purchased? This also generated questions about consumerism in Cuba and its relationship to possible growing disenchantment with the regime. Wald indicated that most families had refrigerators. Some got them at workplaces, with those voted best workers getting first choice. There was a credit system in Cuba and low interest rates. Also Cubans had much discretionary income because of low prices and free services for basic needs. Since rents could not exceed six percent of income and similar caps existed for basic utility rates, and since medical care and education were free, Cubans could save many pesos to purchase expensive items, especially when, as was often the case, there were several income earners living in the same household. Wald said she knew of some Cuban teenagers who paid 120 pesos for blue jeans, roughly $120. While neither she nor her audience could countenance such a cost, she said the teenagers really wanted the jeans and had saved their money for the purchase.

Among those young Cubans who expressed a desire to leave for Miami, and there were many, the sole motivation was economic. These young people, she said, had the erroneous idea that Miami was a land of milk and honey.

As to day-to-day complaints, Wald said that Cubans are most annoyed by bad service and a burdensome bureaucracy. For her, the greatest inconvenience was an unpredictable and inefficient telephone system. She said that some Cubans just worked to get by as work quotas and demands were modest. Until rectification, Cubans had total job protection, which meant that they could not be fired or punished for cause.

In her 1991 briefing, Wald noted that the United States periodically organized "campaigns," or propaganda wars to distort the Cuba story. On her various speaking tours in the U.S. she would receive the same sorts of questions ("Are Cubans drug trafficking?" "Don't Cubans persecute gays?") After being barraged with the latest campaign questions, she would return to Cuba to investigate the issues raised.

As to the drug issue, Cubans did not have them. Anecdotally, she noted that her luggage was never examined by U.S. customs when she returned to the U.S. This was so because the U.S. knows that there are no drugs on the island. Cubans have a historical antipathy for drugs, based upon their perception that drugs were a part of U.S. neocolonialism. Contrary to U.S. claims, Cuba does stop boats in their waters that are transmitting drugs from South America. Most U.S. citizens who are in Cuban jails were convicted of being drug dealers.

The recent trial and sentence to death of revolutionary hero General Ochoa served as a major source of embarrassment to the regime and gave fuel to the U.S. claims of Cuba's complicity in drug trafficking. According to Wald, the trial and the issues it raised were wrenching for the Cuban people. Despite the complicity of Ochoa and high officials of the Interior Ministry, Castro was unaware of the drug smuggling and other transgressions by the conspirators. The reason that the criminals were able to engage in smuggling for eighteen months without getting caught was because the personnel involved were officially assigned the task of engaging in secret trade through Panama to break the U.S. blockade. Consequently, their covert operations were never subjected to the kind of oversight that would have exposed the illegal activities.

Ultimately Ochoa and some of his co-conspirators were sentenced to death. The death sentences were not for the drug offenses but for treason. Ochoa and the others had compromised the country in the eyes of the international community and, most importantly, had given the United States an excuse to invade Cuba.

Karen Wald, in 1991, addressed the critical question of Cuba's adaptation to the radical political and economic changes in the international system. She reported that several of her Cuban friends were optimistic about the economic changes in Cuba. She said that if Cuba survived for the next two to five years, it would be better off than ever before. This was so because the Cubans would have achieved a level of self-sufficiency that had not been reached during the last thirty years.

Cubans were working toward food self-sufficiency and the elimination of inefficiencies. Cuba was being forced to free itself from the socialist division of labor that had consigned it to the production of sugar for COMECON. Along with agricultural self-sufficiency, Cuba was concentrating on building its tourist industry, an export oriented biotechnology industry, pharmaceuticals, and the development of a medical services infrastructure, such as bringing foreigners with special health problems to Cuba for treatment, to earn foreign exchange. Cuba in 1991 had trade and diplomatic relations with more countries than ever before.

While generally supportive of the new economic policies, Cubans were wary of tourism, which one of our Cuban hosts referred to as "our chemotherapy." The Cuban leadership did not fear the introduction of foreign ideas, such as consumerism, resulting from tourism, but did worry about the resentment that Cubans had toward tourists who received special privileges and luxuries unavailable to their own citizens. Tourism contradicted the profoundly egalitarian ideology of the revolution. However, tourism was providing the most immediate source of foreign exchange to substitute for the dissolution of the Socialist Bloc trading system.

As to the 1991 material conditions of life in Cuba, Wald said that "Cubans are the most spoiled people in the world," compared to other Third World peoples. Even in the depths of the current crisis, Cubans were better off. The level of scarcity still included a basic diet, free medical care, and free education. Indeed, Cubans were waiting in long lines for scarce commodities but they were still getting the basics for sustenance. Also, most Cubans were worried about what would happen to the basic provisions of life if the Miami Cubans did return to the island, destroying their economy and expropriating public property.

Wald said that when the regimes in Eastern Europe began to fall, Cuban young people were the first to come out in the streets to demonstrate their commitment to the revolution. The young have been especially supportive of the idea of continuing the one-party system, an idea that was first promulgated by Jose Martí. Large numbers of young people, and most Cubans of all age groups, believe in the right of self-determination and therefore wish to remain independent of all outside influences whether from the United States or socialist states. In sum, most Cubans, and a high percentage of the young, were committed nationalists.

Lastly, Wald spent time discussing Cuba's AIDS policy, the source of considerable controversy. Cubans regarded the AIDS problem as a matter of life and death. Consequently, from 1986 they engaged in a national campaign to test for AIDS and to institutionalize those who had the disease. In subsequent years, treatment and oversight of AIDS patients eased considerably. AIDS patients in the sanitarium received the best medical care possible including access to the latest drugs. Not all AIDS patients were institutionalized as they once were.

Wald also reported that homophobia which, of course, preceded the revolution in Cuba, was declining The government had a national sexual education program which conceptualized homosexuality as an alternative life style, not a disease. While people of the same gender may not marry, they could adopt children. Still, however, homosexuals could not join the Cuban Communist Party. Policies regarding homosexuals as well as other policies suggested that while the revolution had made enormous progressive strides, it still had to push ahead to completely revolutionize the old order.

Briefing by a Cuban Economist

Shortly before the end of our 1991 visit, we spent an evening with Carlos Tablada, noted Cuban economist who wrote *Che Guevara: Economics and Politics in the Transition to Socialism.* He is an associate of Cuba's Center for the Study of the Americas and of the Center for Research on the World Economy. Tablada made a three-hour presentation, and his response to questions was animated, militant, optimistic, and revolutionary.

He grounded current Cuban economic problems in the history of U.S./Cuban relations. As a result of the 1959 revolution Cuba for the first time was an independent country, independent from domination of Spain or the United States. Since the United States refused to honor this new status, policies were established to isolate the new government. In this context the Cuban government had no choice but to respond positively to the offer of assistance from the Soviet Union and Eastern European countries. And despite the radical changes today in the once Socialist countries and their relationship to Cuba, Cubans will remain eternally grateful to them for their support in those difficult moments of the revolution's history.

Having praised the solidarity of the former socialist bloc, Tablada indicated that the shift towards the Soviet economic model by Cuba was not universally endorsed by Cuba's leaders. In fact, Tablada claimed that Fidel Castro and Che Guevara had misgivings about Cuba adopting the Soviet model of economic development. However, by the early 1970s Cuba became fully integrated into COMECON and assumed its role of producing sugar, nickel, and citrus fruits as part of the socialist division of labor. At the time the Socialist countries were developing at a regular pace and were stable politically. Cuba, too, developed and by comparison with other Latin American countries—even the more advanced ones, like Mexico, Argentina, and Venezuela—more successfully provided for its people.

As a result of reflection on Cuba's errors, the government began to rethink its policies in 1984 and by 1986 had embarked upon a rectification campaign that was totally independent from and preceded the Gorbachev reforms. Central to rectification were the principles that Cuba would have to produce what it could profitably produce at home for its own use, that Cuba had to produce what was needed to survive the embargo, and that the Cuban economy could not be isolated from the world. Also Cuba remained committed to providing on an equal basis as many products to the people as possible, and any privileges and inequities that occurred as a result of the policies of the period from 1970 to 1984 would be ended.

Tablada was asked to elaborate on those elements of the Soviet model that were mistakes, some of which influenced Cuban policy. He listed several. First, there was an overreliance on the production of sugar, nickel, and citrus, a Socialist division of labor that impaired the building of self-reliance. Second, the workers, in the Soviet case, while owning the means of production were not made to feel that fact. The social relations of production remained much like in capitalist systems. Hence, working people in the Soviet Union were precluded from active participation in decision making. Of course, Tablada claimed, despite its flaws, Soviet socialism "took civilization" to over 100 countries in the international system. And the Soviets themselves had developed out of extreme backwardness and built socialism in a country where there was 98 percent illiteracy at the time of the Bolshevik Revolution. Therefore, the Soviet model erred by not fully including democracy in its socialism. The Soviet model ultimately stifled the capacity to change and adapt to new circumstances.

Another mistake in the Soviet model was its dogmatic and schematic application of Marxism/Leninism. Marxism/Leninism is really the first step in historical transformation, not the last. Consequently, Soviet leaders were unable to adapt to crises in their own society because they had a fixed conception of their world, said Tablada. The Cuban model was based upon mass participation and mobilization. When it became clear that day-care centers were needed to care for children of working parents in Havana, Fidel went to the people and explained the problem. People mobilized in microbrigades then constructed over 100 such centers in two years to satisfy the need. The program could not have been successful without the active and willing role of the people.

Therefore, Tablada suggested that despite the vital role the Soviet Union and Eastern Europe played in the ability of Cuba to survive U.S. aggression, the Soviet model applied to Cuba's economic and political development had long-term negative consequences for Cuba's ability to maintain its self-determination. Realizing this, the rectification campaign to overcome these flaws was initiated and is still in process in Cuba. Ultimately, the rectification campaign is seeking to reinvigorate the "Cuban Model" of social and economic development; a model that emphasizes planning, decentralization, a diversified economy, democracy, and human need fulfillment. While the Cuban model is experiencing its gravest crisis since the fall of the Socialist Bloc, Tablada remained the most optimistic among Cubans and North Americans who briefed us about its future. For him, only one model of socialism was in crisis, but socialism itself was not in crisis.

Briefings By Foreign Affairs Specialists, Cuban Communist Party

During our two visits we received briefings by foreign affairs specialists of the Americas Department, Division of International Affairs, of the Cuban Communist Party. The primary spokesperson was Juan Antonio Blanco in 1990 and he and Fernando Garcia in 1991. Both had experience as diplomats in the United States and as professors at the University of Havana.

The 1991 briefing was particularly intense; it covered a broad range of subjects for over five and one-half hours. The issues discussed included Cuba's response to the changing character of the international system, economic policy, participation and change in the Communist Party, dissent in Cuba, human rights, the status of Afro-Cubans and women in Cuban society, nuclear power, and what U.S. citizens interested in a changed policy toward Cuba can do to ease the crisis that Cuba is experiencing.

First, Blanco and Garcia analyzed the place of Cuba in the new international system. This involved an assessment of the global capitalist system, the special and hostile U.S./Cuban relationship, the relationship of Cuba to other Third World countries, and Cuba's relationship to progressive forces around the world. As to the first layer of reality, Blanco said, Cuba finds itself as an island of socialism in a sea of capitalism. Therefore Cuba, in a world of international capitalist production, had to maintain socialist production at home without the traditional bases of support from elsewhere. Also, Cuba had to sustain a counter-culture to forestall the global culture of capitalism; a culture that resists capitalist values and maintains socialist values of solidarity and egalitarianism. However, this counter-culture and alternative economic system had to be maintained without further isolating Cuba from the world community. The dilemma was how this island nation could sustain its economic, political, and cultural independence in the new international system.

A second reality for Cuba involved the special relationship Cuba had with the capitalist hegemonic power, the United States. The Cuban revolution was a socialist one and consequently, to survive must sustain its socialist character. However, the United States, for its part, was demanding an end to socialism in Cuba in exchange for better relations. Consequently, the United States was opposing all negotiations with Cuba.

Ultimately, the motivation for U.S. policy, Blanco asserted, was not anti-communism but rather the Monroe Doctrine. The end of the Cold War did not mean that an end to U.S./Cuban hostilities was to be expected. The United States wanted control over Cuba and by its acts had indicated that it opposed any efforts at real independence in the Western Hemisphere—as reflected in U.S. responses in the 1970s to the Allende regime in Chile and the Manley government in Jamaica.

Currently, the United States was tightening the economic blockade and was increasing psychological warfare against Cuba. This meant that Cuba was of necessity in a wartime situation. U.S. propaganda was being generated to convince Cubans and Third World supporters of Cuba that socialism meant scarcity. The rationing system in Cuba, in place since 1962, was designed to equally distribute society's resources but the U.S. then as now interprets rationing as evidence that rationing means suffering.

The U.S. is trying to project an image to Cubans of a capitalist utopia in which everyone can have a North American middle-class lifestyle.

Concerning specific economic manifestations of the current period of crisis that Cuba was experiencing, four factors were of acute importance: three of these were external and one was internal. As to the former, Cuban economic life was constrained by the international debt (and with U.S. pressure, the reticence of international financial agencies to provide Cuba with loans), falling prices for Cuban export commodities such as sugar, and the economic blockade.

The internal factor most shaping Cuba's problems involved errors and inefficiencies. Cuba had to find new technologies that were not wasteful and new markets for the goods it produced. In the first half of 1991 Cuba had acquired (from overseas and domestic production) one million tons of oil but it typically consumed ten million tons per year. While joint ventures in the tourist sector continued, the U.S. was increasingly pressuring the French, the Spanish, the Germans and others to end these joint ventures.

As to the residues of the Socialist trading bloc, Blanco reported that he had just heard of decisions by the Soviet Union and its former Eastern European allies to resume trade with each other. He said that this was probably required by the fact that the COMECON countries did not produce goods competitive with the West and consequently would not have customers if not with each other.

Regarding Cuba's traditional relationship with the countries of the South, through the non-aligned movement and in the United Nations, severe constraints existed. Most Third World nations were forced by the IMF, the World Bank, and industrial capitalist countries to adopt the so-called "neoliberal" economic development model. This model required declining public services, increased profits to foreign investment, constraints on workers' and peasants' wages, benefits, and social safety nets, and allocation of resources on the basis of the market.

The net effect of neoliberalism has been that Third World countries were more dependent on the core capitalist countries and their banks, were poorer than ever, and were more divided than ever. Even the so-called Third World democracies supported the status quo. Consequently the non-aligned movement had weakened, delegates to international organizations no longer called for a New International Economic Order, and groups of countries did not meet together to develop common bargaining strategies on the debt issue. In short, Cuba's traditional allies in the Third World were much weaker and more vulnerable than before, which reduced the prospects of joint action in the future.

On the issue of international solidarity among progressive forces, while the international communist movement had dissipated, broader groupings of progressives had begun to meet to coordinate activities on an international basis. Early in 1991 Blanco attended an international conference of progressives in Europe. The attendees included socialists, greens, representatives of women's groups, etc. Daniel Ortega, the Sandinista delegate, called for the creation of a new international movement that would organize around the various progressive issues. Since then, a conference of progressive parties was held in Brazil and in June a similar meeting was to be held in Mexico. Other examples of international solidarity involved collaboration between trade unionists from several countries whose membership worked in the same multinational corporations. These efforts were designed to coordinate strategies in response to the global policies of their multinational corporations.

After discussing Cuba and the international system, the briefers responded to questions about domestic politics. They began with a discussion about debate in preparation for the Fourth Party Congress of the Cuban Communist Party (held in October, 1991). In the year prior to the congress, Cubans had been urged to participate in discussions of issues critical to Cuba's future, including the one-party state, tourism, religious believers in the party, the market etc. People engaged in dialogue in popular organizations as well as in local Party bodies. Debates were often carried on television as well.

A party unit of 15 to 20 people might have spent twenty hours in debate on a given subject. Opinions resulting from these grassroots discussions were tabulated such that leaders had a sense of what their members felt. In 1990 and 1991, the discussion process had involved extensive debate in some 80,000 assemblies around the country.

Cubans in the assemblies, and later at the Fourth Party Congress, endorsed the continuation of the one-party system. Blanco pointed out that the need for a single revolutionary party was conditioned by circumstance and history. The one-party vision that animated Cubans was not derived from socialist theory but rather the ideas of José Martí, who saw a single party, with much internal debate, as required by the threats from colonial and neo-colonial powers on Cuba's independence. Blanco reminded the delegates that the United States did not develop a two-party system until 1796, twenty years after the revolution. Major stalwarts of the U.S. revolution such as George Washington and Benjamin Franklin opposed a two-party system.

In response to a question about debate within the university, Garcia and Blanco claimed that controversial issues were explored. Those few from the university who had been disciplined had been punished not for their views but because of their counterrevolutionary activities. Blanco pointed out that there was a historic relationship between instances of domestic repression and the threat of U.S. aggression; the greater the threat, the harsher the limitations on the activities of critics. However even in the 1970s, dissent was not punished in the fashion ascribed to Eastern Europe and elsewhere.

Blanco indicated that as a professor of philosophy at the university, he objected to the adoption of rigid Soviet Marxist texts in the curriculum. His views were not accepted and he left the university, but took up his current position with the international relations department of the Cuban Communist Party.

He claimed that Cuban students today wanted more Marxism in their curriculum, not less, but a Marxism of a more sophisticated nature, not a formulaic and dogmatic Marxism.

Addressing the issue of human rights, they noted that there were no "disappeared" in Cuba, no police riots, no instances of torture. Human rights included social and economic rights as well as political rights. In many societies, the structure of life constitutes a daily violation of human rights as hunger, disease, and ignorance abound. Similarly, some countries such as El Salvador daily violate political rights of their citizens, as well as violate the social and economic rights. Cuba did neither.

They recalled the U.S. campaign in the 1980s to condemn Cuban prisons. Despite Cuba's refusal to allow unchecked inspections by outsiders, because this intrinsically violates national sovereignty, Cuba allowed delegations of North Americans to visit Cuban prisons. In one case, Cuba agreed to visits if in turn the U.S. observers would try to secure Cuba's right to visit U.S. prisons. Of course, the U.S. refused to grant such a request.

In 1984 and 1985, representatives of Amnesty International and America's Watch visited Cuban prisons. However, in their subsequent publications they did not emphasize as much what they saw as they did the claims made by Cuba's critics. Ironically, Cuban citizens were calling for longer jail sentences and more repression rather than less. However, Blanco said, Cuba had a long tradition of correct treatment of prisoners going back to the days of the revolution and the Bay of Pigs. Despite U.S. claims, Cubans had a strong sense of justice.

They discussed issues of racism and sexism in Cuban society. Concerning racism, the speakers referred to the major Afro-Cuban critic of Cuban society, Carlos Moore. They pointed out that he had not been in Cuba since 1963 and he surfaced later in the United States as an "expert" on race relations in Cuba. Contrary to Moore's charges, there were no problems of racism against Afro-Cubans today. To Garcia and Blanco, there were no minorities, whether racial or ethnic. Ironically, the U.S. administration was praising itself for the role of an Afro-American general, Colin Powell, when Afro-Cuban generals had played significant military roles throughout Cuba's history.

While claiming a virtual end to racism in Cuba, the speakers indicated that patterns of sexual discrimination still remained. Sexism remained a significant problem in Cuban society. Despite the Family Code, women still did two jobs; one at the factory or worksite, the other at home. This double burden made it exceedingly difficult for women to assume significant roles in popular organizations or the Party. Hence, women were less likely to be in leadership positions. Some laws presumed to benefit women, such as released time for various child care functions. However, men then claimed that women should wait in the food lines because they had been "privileged" by released time. One hope for the future was that each new generation was more flexible than its predecessor (hopefully both men and women).

They were asked to comment on the recent U.S. crusade to condemn Cuba's nuclear power plant construction. They indicated that nuclear power was problematic everywhere but Cuba's oil dependency coupled with dwindling supplies made it necessary to expand nuclear power. Without nuclear power and oil, Cubans would starve. Nuclear and oil as sources of energy are transitional until such time as the world crisis is over. It was noted that Cuba was bringing the safest possible technology to the new nuclear projects (in no way comparable to Chernobyl). Cuba invited others, including U.S. Congresspersons, to inspect the Cuban facilities. Of course, such an open invitation should be granted Cuba by the United States to visit nuclear power plants in Florida.

After a long and information-filled briefing, delegates left with a sense of determination to return to the U.S. and work to reverse its imperial policies toward this island nation.

The Delegations Take A Stand

While most of the delegates had been sympathetic to the Cuban Revolution at the outset of the trips, the variety of experiences and discussions with Cubans increased their commitment to support the revolution. First, delegates to both conferences issued carefully worded resolutions derived from extensive debate calling on the United States government to change its policy toward Cuba. We urged our government to end the economic blockade, the limitations on cultural relations, and the threat of military action. We called for a normalization of relations, claiming that such a change would be advantageous to both countries.

Resolutions were read to press conferences and members of our delegations were interviewed in the Cuban media. We were told that the expressions of support buoyed the spirits of Cubans during their time of crisis.

Further, delegates discussed among themselves and Cuban friends a variety of activities that they could engage in back in the United States. Delegates committed themselves to write editorials and letters to the editor in their local newspapers, agreed to sponsor public speaking events for Cubans and others to discuss Cuba and United States policy, and discussed plans for forthcoming academic conferences in Cuba and ways to bring Cuban scholars to the United States. Some agreed to organize the sending of academic books to help overcome shortages in the university and others discussed organizing shipments of medical supplies. Delegates talked about a variety of solidarity groups in the United States who were urging their Congresspeople to change the laws regarding Cuba.

We all recognized that with the collapse of the Socialist Bloc, the new U.S. drive to regain its global hegemony, and rekindled U.S. militarism as manifested in Panama and Iraq, the task of reversing U.S. policy toward Cuba would be very difficult. We also were cognizant of the life and death struggle Cuba was experiencing in the 1990s. While we could not predict the outcome of Cuba's struggle for survival, we knew that we had to use our words and deeds to the best of our abilities in support of Cuba's right to national self-determination.

A cartoon painted on the wall of a building describes what the U.S.-deployed "TV—Marti" is broadcasting to the Cuban people.

Chapter 7

Cuba's Past; Cuba's Future

The Fourth Congress of the Cuban Communist Party was held in October, 1991. Initially, before the crisis in socialism, it was envisioned that the Congress would evaluate the progress of the rectification campaign which was set in motion during the Third Party Congress in 1986. While this still was on the agenda, the Congress was forced by historical circumstance to examine the rectification process in the light of the severe economic and political crisis brought about by the collapse of the Socialist countries; what the Cubans call "the special period." Now Cubans had to examine programs old and new from the perspective of saving the revolution itself.[1]

With that fundamental issue in mind, 1,667 delegates to the Congress deliberated for five full days and agreed to a set of policies to defend the revolution. The assembly elected new members to the Central Committee of the Party and approved six substantive resolutions to support rectification and defend the revolution.[2]

The Congress endorsed the need for an environment within the party that was free of discrimination of any kind so that open debate could occur. Consequently, it voted to allow religious believers to become members of the Communist Party. Further, it was resolved that the Party should act to reinforce the independence of state organs and the mass organizations so as to reduce the direct control of the Party on Cuban life.

The Congress called on the Central Committee to draw up a program of new priorities for Cuba, as the 1986 Congress had done. It warned against past errors of mechanistically following policies and programs of other countries rather than developing programs based upon Cuba's history and needs. The priorities of the rectification campaign were reviewed and achievements between 1986 and 1990 were noted—such as the construction boom, the renewal of voluntary labor, and efforts at streamlining the economy.

The Congress voted to have representatives to the national legislature elected by direct secret ballot, rather than selected by municipal and provincial representatives. Also the Congress urged that greater powers be given to the municipal assemblies and the procedures for recalling representatives be loosened.

The Congress prioritized economic tasks for the special period. The first task was to work toward food self-sufficiency. Programs to support the most successful foreign exchange earners such as tourism and medical exports were continued as high priorities. Also, the Congress acted to encourage foreign investment, especially by Latin American business persons. Finally, specified forms of self-employment, particularly in services, were endorsed.

A resolution on foreign policy called for an end to the U.S. economic blockade and an end to the U.S. military occupation at Guantanamo. It declared Cuba's willingness to sign a regional nuclear non-proliferation treaty. Further, the resolution called for a democratized United Nations and demanded that each nation be given the right to choose its own form of government.

The last resolution changed the character of the Central Committee, strengthening it and at the same time making it more representative of the Cuban people. Members would be drawn from the 48,000 branches of the party and would be full members, with the status of alternate member eliminated. Fifty-six percent of those elected to the Central Committee by secret ballot were new. They tended to be better educated than the prior Central Committee, were less likely to be long-time party cadre and had spent less years in the party. The Political Bureau elected by the Central Committee had 14 new members of the 25 seated.[3]

The basic character of the Congress was to continue the efforts at economic self-sufficiency, democratization, mass participation, and mass mobilization that were the hallmark of the rectification campaign. Some structural changes in the Party were made and policies to increase the attractiveness of Cuba to foreign investors were recommended. The central task, as the Congress saw it, was to defend the revolution in this time of crisis.[4]

Historical Continuities and Changes

As the preceding pages suggest, there have been many changes in the Cuban experience since 1959 and yet other features of the revolution remain the same. In some cases changes occurred over the years since 1959 only to be reversed in the recent past.

First, what has not yet changed from the historic past is Cuba's dependence on sugar as its major foreign exchange earner. The sugar economy that was established by the Spanish remains today despite the radical shift away from external dependence over the last two years. As Karen Wald suggested, the contemporary crisis Cuba is experiencing may be the required stimulus needed to end the historic dependency on sugar once and for all. To a significant degree, the survival of the revolution will depend upon its ability to overcome the sugar economy.

Second, despite enormous changes and advances since 1959, Cuba remains part of the Third World, a world which has been shaped and distorted in its economics and politics by the global capitalist system and its leading actors. Cuba, while in many ways a developed and even industrialized country, remains closer in economic profile and diplomatic standing and possibility to the nations of Asia, Africa, and Latin America than the industrial capitalist countries of North America, Europe, and Japan. In C.Wright Mills' words Cuba remains part of the "hungry bloc," not in the sense of poverty and scarcity as he meant it—Cuba is part of the First World in these terms—but in the sense of still struggling to achieve its right and capacity to define its own destiny. In fact, it could be argued that Cuba's "hunger" for self-determination, its spirit of nationalism, is what drives the revolution in 1991, as it drove the revolution in 1959, and 1933, and 1898, and 1868.

In addition to continuities with Cuba's pre-revolutionary past, there are others that should be noted in the period of the revolution, 1959 to the present. The most obvious one is the hatred and aggressive stance of the United States. This stance has been driven by the needs and hopes of capitalism, the fears of communism, the racism of assuming the right to control "our backyard," the Monroe Doctrine, and the lenses of Realpolitic that claim the Western Hemisphere as part of the United States sphere of influence.

In Cuba since 1959 there has been a high level of support for the revolution because it provided substantial economic advances for the people and satisfied their thirst for self-determination. Consequently—even though this special period is one in which some of these advances are being reversed—support, while declining somewhat, is holding because the revolution satisfied the spirit of nationalism for the vast majority of the Cuban people.

Finally, a continuous element of the Cuban revolution has been change and a pragmatic spirit that addresses needs, possibilities, and dangers as they arise. As has been repeated often throughout this text, Cuba has been one vast laboratory experiment in which new policies, priorities, and programs have been introduced to meet the exigencies of the moment. Alongside the dogmatisms and bureaucratic resistances has been the willingness of Cubans to throw out the old, the unworkable, the threatened, and replace it with the new as history requires.

The revolution has brought remarkable changes from before 1959. These are what are most talked about in reference to Cuba. The revolution ended foreign ownership of the Cuban economy. It created an egalitarian society, both in ideology and in fact. It provided health care, education, jobs, and a rich cultural life to all Cubans.

At the most fundamental level, the revolution fulfilled all of the goals Fidel Castro articulated in his 1953 "History Will Absolve Me" speech. For most Cubans alive before 1959, there is no question that the revolution has been an outstanding success. This is true for their sons and daughters if one could compare their possibilities before 1959 with what they have achieved afterwards. The qualitative improvement in the quality of life is most stark when comparing the lives of the people in the rural areas before 1959 and today. The revolution has worked.

And last, there is one significant change from the period between 1959 and 1990 and today. For 31 years the Cuban revolution was supported by a Socialist Bloc which, for all its faults, provided aid, trade partners, and deterrence from external aggression that allowed the revolution to flower and grow. The Soviet Union was not a new power making Cuba dependent like

Spain or the United States before it; the Soviet alliance allowed the Cuban revolution to achieve some measure of independence in a world in which the Colossus of the North was plotting the downfall of the revolution from just 90 miles away. After 31 years of support, the Cuban revolution must now find a way to survive without the support of the once-powerful Soviet Union and its allies.

What Needs to Be Done

This essay began with a discussion of Cuba as metaphor. With the collapse of the Socialist Bloc and the discrediting of one vision of socialism because of the former's failures, progressive people, poor people, people of color, women, workers, students, elderly persons, ecologists have been stripped of the historical ideal that has animated countless millions to act on behalf of social change. Cuba, leave aside appropriate criticisms of its performance, remains the repository of that vision that has inspired peoples since the industrial revolution. In that sense, the Cuban revolution is the revolution of all who commit themselves to progressive social change. Consequently, the Cuban revolution must be defended.

At the time of this writing, the defense of Cuba necessitates that concerned U.S. citizens march, rally, write to newspapers, and communicate with Congresspersons to demand that U.S. foreign policy change. The economic blockade must end. The military threat must end. The Guantanamo base must be shut down. The right of U.S. citizens to travel to Cuba must be reinstated. A serious effort must be undertaken by the U.S. government to reestablish normal diplomatic relations, cultural exchanges, scientific and technological collaboration, and even to allow U.S. investment on Cuban soil.

The Cold War is over. Cuba is not a threat to the United States. And most importantly, Cuba has the right to determine its own destiny not dictated by any outside power. National self-determination and social justice have been the twin pillars of the revolutionary struggle ever since the Spanish landed on the island, and have remained the driving passion until today. Cubans, progressives around the world, and concerned U.S. citizens must all work together to defend Cuba's right to develop its revolution.

The World Situation

The U.S. has everyone by the balls
        at the present time,

just like the Medes,
the Persians,
the Greeks,
the Romans,
the Egyptians,
and the Mongols

      did in their turn....

June 12, 1991   *Bob Randolph*

NOTES

CHAPTER 2

1. Louis A. Perez, Jr. *Cuba; Between Reform and Revolution*, New York: Oxford, 1988. Hugh Thomas, *Cuba: The Pursuit of Freedom*, New York: Harper and Row, 1971.

2. Donald W. Bray and Timothy F. Harding, "Cuba," in Ronald H. Chilcote and Joel C. Edelstein, *Latin America: The Struggle With Dependency and Beyond*, Cambridge: Schenkman, 1974, 586-587.

3. Perez, 86-87.

4. Bray and Harding, 586-587.

5. Perez, 109.

6. Bray and Harding, 591.

7. "The Platt Amendment" in Philip Brenner, William M. LeoGrande, Donna Rich, and Daniel Siegel ed. *The Cuba Reader: The Making of a Revolutionary Society*, New York: Grove Press, 1989, 30-31.

8. Bray and Harding, 593-596.

9. Leo Huberman and Paul M. Sweezy, *Cuba: Anatomy of a Revolution*, New York: Monthly Review, 1960, 22.

10. Bray and Harding, 604.

11. David Horowitz, *The Free World Colossus*, New York: Hill and Wang, 1971, 198-200.

CHAPTER 3

1. Leo Huberman and Paul M. Sweezy, *Cuba; Anatomy....* Joseph North, *Cuba: Hope of a Hemisphere*, New York: International Publishers, 1961. C. Wright Mills, *Listen, Yankee: The Revolution in Cuba*, New York: McGraw-Hill, 1960.

2. Huberman and Sweezy, xi.

3. Huberman and Sweezy, 3-7.

4. Huberman and Sweezy, 22.

5. Huberman and Sweezy, 10.

6. Huberman and Sweezy, 37.

7. Huberman and Sweezy, 38.

B. Huberman and Sweezy, 42-43.

9. Huberman and Sweezy, 73.

10. Huberman and Sweezy, 79-81.

11. Huberman and Sweezy, 171.

12. Huberman and Sweezy, 191.

13. Huberman and Sweezy, 202.

14. Huberman and Sweezy, 175.

15. North, 12-13.

16. North, 13.

17. North, 28.

18. North, 88-89.

19. North, 89.

20. North, 74.

21. North, 94.

22. Mills, 8.

23. Mills, 7.

24. Mills, 29.

25. Mills, 31.

26. Mills, 45.

27. Mills, 26.

28. Mills 114.

29. Mills, 116.

30. Mills, 155.

31. Mills, 179.

CHAPTER 4

1. Carmelo Mesa-Lago, "Revolutionary Economic Policies in Cuba," in Philip Brenner, William M. LeoGrande, Donna Rich, and Daniel Siegel ed. *The Cuba Reader: The Making of a Revolutionary Society*, New York: Grove, 1989, p. 63.

2. Mesa-Lago, 69.

3. Donald W. Bray and Timothy F. Harding, *op. cit.*, 623-24.

4. Edward Boorstein, *The Economic Transformation of Cuba*, New York: Monthly Review, 1968.

5. Ernesto "Che" Guevara, "Man and Socialism in Cuba," in Philip Brenner, William M. LeoGrande, Donna Rich, and Daniel Siegel ed. *The Cuba Reader*: 83-89.

6. Mesa-Lago, 74.

7. Wassily Leontief, "1970 and the Trouble With Cuban Socialism," in Philip Brenner, William M. Leo-Grande, Donna Rich and Daniel Siegel, The Cuba Reader: 101-102.

8. William M. LeoGrande, "Party Development in Revolutionary Cuba," in Philip Brenner, William M. LeoGrande, Donna Rich, and Daniel Siegel ed. *The Cuba Reader*: 156-160.

9. William M. LeoGrande, 160-163.

10. William M. LeoGrande, 163-169.

11. William M. LeoGrande, "Mass Political Participation in Socialist Cuba," in *The Cuba Reader*: 187.

12. Wayne S. Smith, *The Closest of Enemies*, New York: Norton, 1987, 13-43.

13. Morris H. Morley, *Imperial State and Revolution: The United States and Cuba, 1952-1986*, London: Cambridge, 1987,178-240.

14. Morley,135-146.

15. Morley, 178-240.

16. Graham T. Allison, *Essence of Decision; Explaining the Cuban Missile Crisis*, Boston: Little, Brown, 1971.

17. Robert A. Pastor, "Cuba and the Soviet Union: Does Cuba Act Alone?" in Philip Brenner, William M. LeoGrande, Donna Rich, and Daniel Siegel ed. *The Cuba Reader: The Making of a Revolutionary Society*, New York: Grove, 1989, 298.

18. William M. LeoGrande, "Cuba's Policy in Africa," in *The Cuba Reader*: 379-384.

19. Donna Rich, "Cuban Internationalism: A Humanitarian Foreign Policy," in *The Cuba Reader*: 405-413.

CHAPTER 5

1. Harry R. Targ, *Strategy of an Empire in Decline: Cold War II*, Minneapolis: MEP, 1986, 181-273.

2. David Holloway, "Gorbachev's New Thinking," *Foreign Affairs*, "America and the World 1988/89," Vol. 68, No. 1, 1989, 66-81.

3. Robert Legvold, "The, Revolution in Soviet Foreign Policy," *Foreign Affairs*, "America and the World 1988/89" Vol. 68, No. 1, 1989, 87.

4. Robert Legvold, 86.

5. Harry R. Targ, 215-223.

6. Harry R. Targ, 229-244.

7. James A. Nathan and James K. Oliver, *United States Foreign Policy and World Order*, third edition, Boston: Little, Brown, 1985, 449.

8. Carolyn C. Perrucci, Robert Perrucci, Dena B. Targ, and Harry R. Targ, *Plant Closings: International Context and Social Costs*, New York: Aldine de Gruyter, 1988, 15-24.

9. Noam Chomsky, "'What We Say Goes':The Middle East in the New World Order," *Z Magazine*, May, 1991, 50.

10. Max Azicri, "The Cuban Rectification: Safeguarding the Revolution While Building the Future," in Sandor Halebsky and John M. Kirk ed., *Transformation and Struggle: Cuba Faces the 1990s*, New York: Praeger, 1990, 3-20.

11. Max Azicri, 9.

12. Sandor Halebsky and John M. Kirk, "Introduction," in Halebsky and Kirk., ed., *Transformation and Struggle*: xi-xxvi.

13. Fidel Castro, "The More Limited Our Resources Become, The More Decisive is Our Understanding of How to Use Them Rationally and Optimally," *Granma International*, May 5, 1991, 13.

14. Fidel Castro, 14.

15. Fidel Castro, 14.

CHAPTER 7

1. Fidel Castro, "The Only Situation in Which We Would Have No Future Would Be If We Lost Our Homeland, the Revolution and Socialism," *Granma International*, November 3, 1991, xvii-xxvii.

2. Gail Reed, "'To Save the Country, the Revolution and Socialism,'" *People's Weekly World*, Saturday, November 2, 1991, 12-13.

3. Gail Reed, 13.

4. "4th Party Congress," *Granma International*, October 20, 1991, i-xii.

Index

9460 = ≡

7